LUDWIG VAN BEETHOVEN

AUTOGRAPH MISCELLANY FROM *CIRCA* 1786 TO 1799

LUDWIG VAN BEETHOVEN

AUTOGRAPH MISCELLANY FROM *CIRCA* 1786 TO 1799

BRITISH MUSEUM ADDITIONAL MANUSCRIPT 29801, ff. 39–162

(THE 'KAFKA SKETCHBOOK')

<hr />

VOLUME I · FACSIMILE

EDITED BY JOSEPH KERMAN

PROFESSOR OF MUSIC, UNIVERSITY OF CALIFORNIA AT BERKELEY

<hr />

LONDON 1970

PUBLISHED BY THE TRUSTEES OF THE BRITISH MUSEUM

WITH THE CO-OPERATION OF THE ROYAL MUSICAL ASSOCIATION

PRINTED IN GREAT BRITAIN
AT THE UNIVERSITY PRESS, OXFORD
BY VIVIAN RIDLER
PRINTER TO THE UNIVERSITY

CONTENTS

PREFACE

NINETY-FIVE years ago—just too late for the first Beethoven centenary celebrations in 1870—the British Museum acquired, for an outlay of £130, its greatest Beethoven treasure, the autograph miscellany of sketches published in the present volumes. In the summer of 1967 the Royal Musical Association conceived the happy idea of proposing to the Museum the publication of a complete facsimile and transcription of the manuscript, to be edited by Professor Joseph Kerman of the University of California at Berkeley. The suggestion was welcomed, and the project was planned with a view to synchronising publication with the opening of the Beethoven Exhibition in the King's Library of the British Museum on 27 November 1970. This exhibition in which the original manuscript here reproduced will naturally have a place of honour, is being further commemorated by the issue of a booklet, *Beethoven and England : an account of sources in the British Museum*, which will describe the various Beethoven manuscripts in the Museum's collections, and review aspects of Beethoven's relations with this country.

Grateful thanks are due to the Royal Musical Association both for initiating the project and assisting in a variety of ways, particularly through Mr. Andrew Porter. To Professor Kerman, whose own personal acknowledgements, in which the Museum would wish to join, appear on p. ix, the Museum and the Royal Musical Association are under an especial obligation for the care and assiduity he has displayed in his very difficult and complex task. The Oxford University Press, who have printed the introduction and plates, and Messrs. Halstan, who have undertaken the setting of the musical transcription, have both collaborated wholeheartedly in producing the volumes to a very tightly planned schedule, while thanks must also be expressed to Messrs. Frank Grunfeld, who have supplied the paper specially manufactured for this edition.

T. C. SKEAT
Keeper of Manuscripts

29 May 1970

ACKNOWLEDGEMENTS

THE planning and preparation of this edition took place in London, California, London, and California again. Therefore special demands were made on those in England who assisted me, demands met with the greatest of patience by members of the British Museum staff and by Mr. Andrew Porter, who provided invaluable help of many kinds. I wish also to express particular appreciation to the President and Council of the Royal Musical Association for their ready encouragement of the project at the planning stage and thereafter.

Professor Joseph Schmidt-Görg, Director of the Beethovenhaus and Beethoven-Archiv, Bonn, and Dr. Hans Schmidt granted me access to the Archive in 1967, and Dr. Schmidt kindly supplied microfilms of supplementary material. Other libraries have provided photographic material or information: the Berlin Staatsbibliothek (Stiftung Preussischer Kulturbesitz, latterly at Tübingen: Dr. Wilhelm Virneisel); Columbia University Library (Mr. Thomas T. Watkins); the Library of Congress (Mr. William Lichtenwanger). My colleague Professor Vincent H. Duckles, Head of the Music Library at the University of California, has been endlessly helpful with services, favours, and expert scholarly advice.

In the preparation of the transcription, Beethoven's writing of words and verbal inscriptions caused me the most uncertainty, and I am therefore especially grateful for assistance in reading this from Professor Blake Spahr, Chairman of the Department of German, University of California, and Dr. Dagmar von Busch-Weise, the editor of several sketchbook editions and probably the foremost authority on Beethoven's handwriting. In the capacity of consultant, Dr. Weise examined photographs of numerous pages, on which she checked readings and supplied lacunae with remarkable skill (ff. 43^v, 48^v, 49^v, $51^{r, v}$, 67^v, 69^v, 86^v, 88^r, 102^v, 111^r, 123^r, 125^v, 127^v, 138^r, 139^v, 153^r, 161^r, and further details on 46^v, 51^r, 66^v, 67^r, 72^v, 75^v, 81^v, 85^r, 98^v, 99^r, 100^r, 106^r, 119^r, 121^r, $122^{r, v}$, 138^v, 141^r, 143^r, 156^v, $157^{r, v}$, 158^r, 159^r). Of the music itself, draft transcriptions and preliminary analyses were prepared in conjunction with graduate students at the University of California, Mrs. Judith Tick Steinberg, Misses Phyllis Kaplan and Margaret Radin, Messrs. Lawrence Brillson, John Conyers, Douglas Johnson, Christopher Macie, and Lee Rosen, in a seminar during 1967–8. Mr. Macie and Miss Charlotte Greenspan then assisted in various stages of the publication. Mr. Johnson, who is engaged in a study of the related manuscript Berlin Aut. 28, has allowed me to make prior use of his transcriptions and findings. Another former student, Professor Sarah Fuller of the State University of New York, Stony Brook, carried out expert research in London on paper characteristics. In a very real sense this has been a joint project with these young scholars; the work would not have gone forward without their participation.

To my friends Professors Elliot Forbes, Jan LaRue, Lewis Lockwood, Mr. O. W. Neighbour, and Dr. Alan Tyson, I have been grateful again and again for information and advice, no less so on the few occasions when I have not felt able to follow their counsel. They must none of them be thought responsible for my own decisions, interpretations, and faults.

J. K.

AUTOGRAPH MISCELLANY FROM *CIRCA* 1786 TO 1799

INTRODUCTION

THE Beethoven Autograph Miscellany here presented in facsimile and transcription comprises 124 sheets in the British Museum Additional Manuscript 29801, ff. 39–162. It was purchased from the composer Johann Nepomuk Kafka in 1875, together with a Beethoven sketchbook of 1811, devoted to studies for *Die Ruinen von Athen* and *König Stephan*.[1] The latter sketchbook now takes up ff. 1–37 of the Additional Manuscript. The miscellany brings together sheets of the period from before 1790, perhaps as early as 1786, to 1798–9. Included are a number of autographs—rough or fair copies of works that Beethoven had completed or meant to complete—as well as a few copies of music by other composers, a mass of sketches, exercises, studies, musical memoranda, and other notations. This great collection was first studied selectively by Gustav Nottebohm, in a number of articles ultimately assembled in his *Beethoveniana* and *Zweite Beethoveniana* of 1872 and 1887, and the whole of it was surveyed in some detail by J. S. Shedlock in *The Musical Times* of 1892.[2] Shedlock's notes formed the basis of the inventory

published in the *Catalogue of Manuscript Music in the British Museum*, 1906–9, by Augustus Hughes-Hughes.[3] Since those times the miscellany has been examined with some frequency by Beethoven scholars, and has been cited regularly in the literature. It is well known as the largest and most important collection of early Beethoven sketch material.

The manuscript is generally identified as the 'Kafka Sketchbook' or 'Kafka Notebook', titles which have little to recommend them beyond convenience of reference. Kafka himself owned the book for only a few years, and in any case also owned other 'Kafka sketchbooks', among them another volume that was acquired by the Museum, Additional Manuscript 29997. More to the point, the manuscript is not a 'sketchbook' in the proper meaning of the term—that is, it is not a single integral work-book transmitting studies for a body of music that was occupying the composer over a limited period of time. As an example, Additional Manuscript 31766 may be cited, one of the better-known sketchbooks as a result of its publication in transcription by the Beethovenhaus at Bonn:[4] this book, dating from the single year 1808, includes some ninety pages of intensive sketching for the Pastoral Symphony, twenty pages for the Piano Trio in D, Op. 70 No. 1, and comparatively little else. By contrast, the sketches contained in the miscellany can be traced to around eighty works (not all of them completed) ranging over a decade, and there is no single movement to which more than six sheets refer. More than one or two sheets is rare. The book is an assemblage of sheets, bifolia, and small gatherings of various different physical characteristics, used over

---

[1] See Gustav Nottebohm, *Beethoveniana*, Leipzig, 1872, pp. 37–44, and his *Zweite Beethoveniana*, ed. Eusebius Mandyczewski, Leipzig, 1887, pp. 14–20, 138–45.

[2] J. S. Shedlock, 'Beethoven's Sketch Books', *Musical Times*, xxxiii (1892), 331, 394, 461, 523, 589, 649 et seq.

[3] ii. 5, 47, 458, 573; iii. 8, 16, 29, 37, 76, 96, 127, 152, 154, 180, 211, 237, 246, 251, 261, 276, 291. The inventory in the *Verzeichnis der Skizzen Beethovens* by Hans Schmidt, *Beethoven-Jahrbuch*, vi (Jg. 1965/8), Bonn, 1969, No. 185, is based mainly on Hughes-Hughes. See also Joseph Kerman, 'Beethoven Sketchbooks in the British Museum', *Proceedings of the Royal Musical Association*, xciii (1967), 94–5.

[4] *Beethoven. Ein Skizzenbuch zur Pastoralsymphonie Op. 68 und zu den Trios Op. 70, 1 und 2*, ed. Dagmar Weise (*Veröffentlichungen des Beethovenhauses in Bonn. Neue Folge. 1. Reihe. Beethoven: Skizzen und Entwürfe: Erste kritische Ausgabe*, iii), Bonn, 2 vols., 1961.

a considerable span of time for writings of various sorts. Most probably the sheets were brought together by Beethoven, but they lack the dense record of continuous work to be found in a sketchbook proper.

The remainder of this introduction consists of a survey of the contents of the miscellany, a brief discussion of its physical characteristics, with a note on the facsimile, and an account of its history, as far as this can be ascertained. Matters concerning the transcription are discussed in the introduction to Volume II.

THE CONTENTS OF THE MISCELLANY: AUTOGRAPHS AND PAGES FROM AUTOGRAPHS.[5] In the following, the word 'autograph' (as a noun) is used to refer to copies of actual compositions, and not taken broadly to include all writings by the composer, such as sketches, small musical memoranda, and the like. But even with the meaning limited in this way, the term is imprecise, and a consideration of the autographs in the miscellany rapidly leads to some problems of definition. On the one hand, there are fair copies made by the composer for presentation or direct transmission to a publisher. On the other, there are manuscripts of a much rougher sort, 'composition drafts' or 'working autographs', which Beethoven seems to have begun at a point when he was finished with preliminary sketching and ready to start writing out the work for the first time. Many details would still be undecided, and so these manuscripts contain many rewritings and corrections; accompaniment figures, repetitions, and so on might be left out at the first writing, to be added later—or never added at all, in the event that the composition was abandoned. At best these manuscripts would generally have been too rough to send to a publisher, though they could have been used by a professional copyist to prepare publishers' copy.

xiv

Around thirty-five sheets of the miscellany—more than a quarter of the total—were originally conceived by Beethoven as autographs of one of these kinds. These sheets have been preserved in a variety of stages of completeness. There are complete autographs; fair copies and working autographs broken off in the middle of a page or left incomplete in other ways; and fragments of one or more pages from longer autographs which have otherwise been lost. In the fragments the accompaniments may or may not be fully written, and we do not always know whether the works were actually finished. In any case, most of the autographs were used over again for sketches and other notations on the blank staffs, so that the forms in which they now reach us are very various, not to say confused. They range from a spotless fair copy with no further additions and few corrections (ff. 107–8, the 'Trinklied', WoO 109) to one case of an abortive autograph broken off after a title, a signature, and seven bars in piano score—whereupon the remaining thirty staffs of the sheet were filled up with miscellaneous matter (f. 66, the Sonatina in G minor, Op. 49 No. 1). The list below is arranged by opus numbers, by 'WoO' (*Werke ohne Opuszahl*) numbers as assigned by the Kinsky-Halm *Das Werk Beethovens: Thematisch-Bibliographisches Verzeichnis*, and by the numbers assigned in Hess, *Verzeichnis der nicht in der Gesamtausgabe veröffentlichten Werke Ludwig van Beethovens*.

Op. 1 No. 2   Piano Trio in G: Scherzo. Allegro. Piano score, broken off after 64 bars. f. 126$^{r, v}$.

Op. 18 No. 5   String Quartet in A: Andante. Incomplete rough score of two rejected variations. f. 152^{r}.

[5] See Lewis Lockwood, 'On Beethoven's Sketches and Autographs: Some Problems of Definition and Interpretation', *Acta Musicologica*, xlii (1970), 32–47, and Alan Tyson, 'Sketches and Autographs', *The Beethoven Companion*, ed. Denis Arnold and Nigel Fortune, London, 1970.

Op. 19	Piano Concerto in B♭: Allegro. Fragment (5 bars) of an early version, in score. f. 89ʳ.
Op. 49 No. 1	Sonatina in G minor for Piano: Andante. Broken off after 7 bars. f. 66ʳ.
Op. 52 No. 2	Feuerfarb' ('Ich weiss eine Farbe'). Fragment (first 15 bars) without words. f. 120ᵛ.
Op. 71	Sextet for Wind Instruments: Menuetto. Quasi allegretto, with trio. ff. 104ᵛ-105ʳ.
WoO 32	Duo for Viola and Violoncello 'mit zwei obligaten Augengläsern'. First movement, complete; beginning of a second movement, broken off after 22 bars—the counterpoint not written in; minuet and trio, complete, on different paper. ff. 135ʳ-137ᵛ, 119ʳ.
WoO 43a	Sonatina in C minor for Mandoline and Piano. Perhaps part of a larger work. f. 87ʳˑ ᵛ.
WoO 65	Variations on 'Venni amore' by Righini, for Piano. Fragment of the early (1790) version (?). f. 123ᵛ.
WoO 109	Trinklied ('Erhebt das Glas'). ff. 107ᵛ-108ᵛ.
WoO 117	Der Freie Mann ('Wer ist ein freier Mann?'). Two slightly different versions, the earlier catalogued as Hess 146. ff. 61ʳ, 62ʳ.
WoO 119	'O care selve' (song). f. 62ᵛ.
Hess 13	Romance: Cantabile. Fragment (first 57 bars) of a movement in E minor from a work for flute, bassoon, and piano with orchestra. ff. 74ᵛ-80ᵛ.
Hess 48	Allegretto in E♭ for Piano Trio. Fragment (the trio is incomplete); presumably part of a larger work. f. 129ʳˑ ᵛ.
Hess 64	Fugue in C for Keyboard. f. 158ʳ.
——	Composition (bagatelle?) in C for Piano. Fragment (first 68 bars), the accompaniment not fully written in. f. 161ᵛ.
——	Composition (fantasia?) in D major/minor for Piano. A long, incomplete working autograph, evidently of a work in three movements: see Vol. II, pp. 285-6. ff. 90ʳ-95ʳ.
——	Composition in G for Orchestra: oboe part. By Beethoven? f. 124ʳ.
——	Duo in E♭ for Violin and Violoncello. Fragment (first 50 bars) of an andantino. f. 130ʳ.
——	Sonata movement in C minor for Piano. Fragment (first 54 bars) of a movement proceeding from grave (?) to allegro, the accompaniment not fully written in. By Beethoven? f. 117ʳ.
——	Symphony in C. Fragment (first 12 bars) of the slow introduction, in score: cf. sketches on ff. 56ʳ-57ᵛ, 127ᵛ-128ᵛ, 158ᵛ-159ᵛ. f. 71ᵛ.

Almost all the works in this list are either *unica* or else otherwise unknown early versions of published works. Hence the importance of the London miscellany in the matter of establishing the Beethoven canon, an importance that is underlined by the rarity of preserved Beethoven autographs from the period before 1800. In addition to these works, which exist in a form that Beethoven must have considered (at least at some stage of the writing) as a 'final' copy, others that are substantially complete appear in a much more haphazard fashion in the midst of other material. There is a piano cadenza for an unknown work in G (ff. 76ᵛ–79ᵛ), a three-part canon in A without words (f. 111ʳ), and a small song, 'Ich sah sie heut', o Liebe' (f. 39ʳ). The manuscript also contains a quantity of minuets, contredanses, and so on, with accompaniments fully or nearly fully specified. But it seems best not to consider these as actual Beethoven 'works', though items of this sort have occasionally been published as such.[6]

The reader will have observed, perhaps with some sense of disappointment, that the twenty-odd works listed above include few of major importance, and some of very small importance. This is not altogether accidental. As will be explained presently, the collection appears to preserve part of a portfolio assembled in early times by Beethoven himself. In later years Beethoven was able and ready to market old compositions; had the portfolio included autographs of music that he considered possible for publication, he might well have taken them out and sent them away to the printers. Indeed, the early Vienna autograph of the song 'Der Freie Mann' on f. 62ʳ bears the numeral 'No 4', referring to the position we know it was to have occupied in a set of songs that Beethoven planned, but failed, to publish in 1803.[7] So the only autographs that remain are minor works, fragments, and superseded versions; the nature of the music preserved is explained by the nature of the source itself. But to look on the bright side, the miscellany is rich in autographs of early works which, if not for this fortuitous means of preservation, would never have become known at all.

SKETCHES AND DRAFTS. The miscellany is of course most famous for its sketches and drafts of early Beethoven compositions. In respect of the works covered, the contents deserve to be called compendious, as appears from the full index on pp. xxxvii ff. This includes about a dozen pieces from the Bonn

xvi

period, before Beethoven moved to Vienna in November 1792, in his twenty-first year. Then from the early Vienna period, all but five works are represented of the first nineteen that were important enough to be published with opus numbers:

Op. 1 Nos. 2 and 3	Piano Trios in G and C minor.
5 Nos. 1 and 2	Sonatas for Violoncello and Piano in F and G minor.
6	Sonata for Piano, Four Hands.
7	Piano Sonata in E♭.
8	Serenade for String Trio.
9 No. 1	String Trio in G.
10 Nos. 2 and 3	Piano Sonatas in F and D.
11	Trio for Clarinet, Violoncello, and Piano.
13	Piano Sonata in C minor ('Pathétique').
14 No. 1	Piano Sonata in E.
15	Piano Concerto No. 1 in C.
16	Quintet for Wind Instruments and Piano.
18 No. 5	String Quartet in A.
19	Piano Concerto No. 2 in B♭.

Sketches also appear for a larger number of works, contemporary with these, that were published later with higher opus numbers, or published in early times without opus numbers, or never published during Beethoven's lifetime at all. These include the Piano Concerto No. 3 in C minor, Op. 37, the Sonatina in G major, Op. 49 No. 2, the Allegretto in C minor for Piano, WoO 53, 'Ah! perfido', Op. 65, and the songs 'Adelaide', Op. 46,

---

[6] *Beethoven. Klavierstücke*, ed. Otto von Irmer, Henle, Munich and Duisburg, 1957, pp. 216–7; *Beethoven. Supplemente zur Gesamtausgabe*, ed. Willy Hess, ix (*Klavierwerke*), Wiesbaden, 1965, pp. 12, 14, 22–4, 26.   [7] Kinsky-Halm, p. 122.

'Das Liedchen von der Ruhe', Op. 52 No. 3, 'Seufzer eines Ungeliebten und Gegenliebe', WoO 118, and the 'Opferlied', WoO 126.

It is well known that Beethoven's sketchbooks contain studies for many works that he never completed. Several dozen such works are sketched here at sufficient length to enable one to form a fair idea of their musical substance, at least as this was taking shape in the composer's mind. Thus the London miscellany opens the door to an extremely interesting shadow world behind the known or knowable world of Beethoven's published music. One of these uncompleted works has received some attention: a Symphony in C which was sketched as early as 1795, and actually scored in part, but then set aside and drawn upon only in 1800 for certain details in the composition of the First Symphony. Discussions of this unfinished symphony, by Nottebohm and Erich Hertzmann, have given no inkling of how very extensive the sketches are, both within the covers of the miscellany and elsewhere.[8] In addition there is an interesting sonata-rondo movement in C minor, perhaps conceived for the Sonate Pathétique; a chamber-music piece for wind instruments and piano with variations on 'Ah, vous dirai-je, maman' as the finale; two fully drafted (if elementary) concerto slow movements; bagatelles, rondos, sonata movements, and at least six songs.

It has already been mentioned that although the miscellany is remarkably rich in the number of works sketched, these are sketched less copiously than is typical of the works found in the true sketchbooks of later periods. For most works or movements, the sketches do not extend beyond one or two pages in transcription. Since the miscellany is not a true sketchbook but a collection of loose sheets, it would be wrong to use it to prove that Beethoven sketched less in early life than later; yet of course almost certainly this must have been the case. Four works appear at greater length: the unfinished sonata movement in C minor and the first movement of the Symphony in C, mentioned above, the rondo of the Piano Concerto in B♭, Op. 19, and the first allegro of the Piano Sonata in E, Op. 14 No. 1. The latter did not escape the sharp eye of Gustav Nottebohm, who singled out this sonata for one of the relatively few *Beethoveniana* articles that sets forth a large mass of sketches for a single work.[9]

A source of wonder even in the composer's lifetime, Beethoven's sketches have in later years been much discussed.[10] It is fair to say that they have acquired the status of a classic topic in musicology, and that few topics in musicology have held out so much interest for musicians who are not primarily scholars. The range of information that it seems possible to wrest from the sketches is notable: they have been used to investigate the chronology of Beethoven's music, its stylistic development, the correct text of certain works, the evolution of individual works and passages, the nature of his creative process, and doubtless other matters. The difficulties of investigation along any of these lines should not be underestimated, and cautions of one kind or another should probably be stressed. Yet the present editor is persuaded that the Beethoven sketches in general—not merely or even principally those in the present collection—constitute a source for study of great potential that has remained largely untapped. Considering the celebrity of this material, it is remarkable how few sketchbooks have been published in usable editions, and how

[8] See Vol. II, pp. 290–1.   [9] *Zweite Beethoveniana*, pp. 45–59.
[10] A good critical survey of the earlier literature on the sketches is provided by Arnold Schmitz in *Beethoven. Unbekannte Skizzen und Entwürfe* (*Veröffentlichungen des Beethovenhauses in Bonn*, iii), Bonn, 1924. The main study is Paul Mies, *Die Bedeutung der Skizzen Beethovens zur Erkenntnis seines Stiles*, Leipzig, 1925 (*Beethoven's Sketches: an Analysis of his Style based on a Study of his Sketch-books*, tr. D. L. Mackinnon, London, 1929).

little serious work has been done with them, whether from the historical, analytical, critical, or psychological points of view. The present edition has been prepared in the main hope of encouraging further study of the sketches by musicians and scholars of varying temperaments and skills, with varying interests in mind.

OTHER NOTATIONS. In addition to autographs, sketches for identifiable works, and notations that give every indication of being sketches for unfinished works, the miscellany includes a mass of notations that give no such immediate indication. These notations are of several kinds, and their function is far from clear. One's first instinct is to regard them as sketches, but on further study it becomes apparent that they should, in fact, be sharply distinguished from sketches proper.

The most characteristic of the various kinds is the small fragment consisting of a few bars in piano score. Whereas in general sketches are written roughly and hastily on one line, with many elisions and omissions, these notations in piano score are often surprisingly neat and complete—down to the clefs, key and time signatures, even tempo indications and dynamics. In contrast to sketches, they are concerned not with linear or thematic development but with piano figuration or texture; they may be founded on a simple alternation of two harmonies, such as tonic and dominant, or on a rigid sequential pattern, diatonic or chromatic. Again in contrast to sketches, which for obvious reasons tend to come in groups, they almost invariably appear in isolation; they are not developed.[11] Sketches record an idea taking shape in the composer's mind, a fleeting moment in a process. But these notations appear to have been written down in relative tranquillity after they were fully formed in Beethoven's mind, or under his fingers. They record something at least temporarily fixed and final.

xviii

The function of these notations in piano score is not clear, as has already been remarked. Many of them look as though they might be imported bodily into Beethoven piano sonatas or variations; but in point of fact not a single one of them has been found to reach such a destination. They might have been designed as basic cells for piano exercises, for the composer or else for his students—a function certainly fulfilled by another smaller category of notations which are provided with remarks about the technical problems addressed. (Nottebohm reprinted some examples of the latter category in the article 'Clavierspiel' in *Zweite Beethoveniana*, pp. 356–63.) The notations of the main kind we are discussing may have been designed as memoranda for improvisations. It seems most likely, however, that they were rather 'improvisations on paper', random ideas about figuration patterns which seem to have come frequently to Beethoven's restless imagination. They may be admitted under the general rubric of compositional studies, but at best they can be considered only as studies in the abstract, to be distinguished from sketches in a concrete situation where a particular work was being composed.

The same must be said for another category of notations, comprising the many minuets, trios, contredanses, *teutschen* or allemandes, and other little tunes scattered throughout the manuscript. Some are complete, some incomplete, some have accompaniments, some do not. Once again, the first instinct is to regard these as sketches for actual ballroom dances to be played at the Vienna Redoutensaal or for sonata minuets and rondos. But surprisingly few turn up in the expected places; and once again the suspicion grows that they must have been studies in the abstract, without any specific destination. Here,

[11] Occasionally they are copied verbatim from one sheet to another: see the note to f. 46, Vol. II, p. 292.

as with the notations in piano score, one has the impression that when he was not sketching actual works in progress, Beethoven liked to keep his hand in, as it were, by writing down whole sets of melodies and pianistic patterns.

That young Beethoven worked in this way does not appear to have been pointed out specifically, though a number of such notations were published as early as 1924 in *Beethoven: Unbekannte Skizzen und Entwürfe*, by Arnold Schmitz. This valuable study includes a facsimile and transcription of Beethovenhaus MS. 114, a bifolium which is very similar in date and character to several in the London miscellany and which indeed may originally have formed part of it. Sketches for the 'Flohlied', Op. 75 No. 3, appear on the inner pages, with all the remaining space filled with miscellaneous notations, nineteen in all. Although only a few look like actual sketches, Schmitz interpreted them all as 'sketches [which] remained uncompleted projects', and he could therefore entertain the hope that one day they might be related to other sketches or even completed Beethoven compositions. This hope is bound to be unfulfilled, both for the Bonn items and for the several hundred similar ones in London.

It is natural to assume that the method of compositional study described here, namely the recording of abstract melodic and figurative ideas, was more common in Beethoven's early life than later. Indeed, there are only a few such notations—though there are some—in the first preserved true sketchbooks, dating from 1798 to 1803, two of which may be studied through editions in complete transcription.[12] Most of the Bonn sheets in the London miscellany contain such notations, and so do many sheets from the earliest Vienna period, 1793–5. Fewer appear on the sheets dating from after 1796 and 1797, the years of Beethoven's extensive concert tours and his somewhat mysterious, but reportedly serious, illness.

These notations are interesting, then, as a record of Beethoven's method of work. They are obviously much less so as musical ideas in themselves. Consideration was given to including in the transcription volume only a selection of them, but it was decided in the end that the problem of selection could not be met satisfactorily and that in any case there was virtue in completeness. Looking at this material *en masse*, the reader is likely to wonder why Beethoven felt impelled to write down so many commonplace notions and then hold on to the sheets of paper for so many years. We should beware, however, of translating this feeling of wonder into a judgement of young Beethoven's musical imagination. This manifested itself in quite another way—in the final concept of works of art, not in memoranda, sketches, or other preliminary studies.

PHYSICAL CHARACTERISTICS. At the British Museum the manuscript was rebound with each separate sheet or bifolium mounted on its own stub or guard, these guards having been cut to suit the size of the pages and produce uniform outer edges for the volume. This method of binding ('guarding in') is habitually used when sheets of different sizes are to be bound together. In cases of original gatherings of two or more bifolia, the inner one is generally still found intact, but the outer ones

---

[12] The earliest true sketchbooks are Berlin Staatsbibliothek, Grasnick 1 and 2 (1798–9: described in *Zweite Beethoveniana*, pp. 476–94), Berlin Aut. 19e (*c.* 1799: see the discussion by Wilhelm Virneisel, 'Aus Beethovens Skizzenbüchern', *Colloquium Amicorum Joseph Schmidt-Görg zum 70. Geburtstag*, ed. Siegfried Kross and Hans Schmidt, Bonn, 1967, pp. 428–31), Landsberg 7 (1800: Karl Lothar Mikulicz, *Ein Notierungsbuch von Beethoven*, Leipzig, 1927), Vienna, Gesellschaft der Musikfreunde, 'Kessler' sketchbook (1801–2: Nottebohm, *Ein Skizzenbuch von Beethoven*, Leipzig, 1865), Glinka Museum, Moscow, 'Wielhorsky' sketchbook (1802–3: N. L. Fishman, *Kniga Eskizov Beethovena Za 1802–1803 Gody*, Moscow, 3 vols., 1962). See *Verzeichnis der Skizzen Beethoven*, Nos. 45, 46, 29, 61, 343.

have been cut for mounting.[13] The manuscript appears to have been put together mostly from single sheets and bifolia: there are the remains of perhaps twelve gatherings of two bifolia each, and of two larger gatherings (seven sheets). At some point, doubtless before the work of the Museum binders, a number of sheets were also cropped, damaged sheets were mended, sometimes clumsily, and a front sheet was added (f. 38).[14]

Of the 248 pages, ten are blank and most of the others are well filled with writing in ink, sometimes in a very fine hand. The ink ranges in colour from black, blue-black, and brown to a faded light grey; red ink appears on one page (f. 62^v), red pencil or crayon on another (f. 106^r), and ordinary pencil on a few others. At the Museum a pencil foliation was added to the recto pages. Within the manuscript a few works have been identified with pencil inscriptions in a foreign hand.

A glance at the facsimile shows how widely the papers differ not only in size but also in colour, staff-ruling, and handwriting. There is a particularly clear contrast between the relatively homogeneous sheets used in Vienna and the twenty-odd Bonn sheets scattered at random through the miscellany; these are irregular in size, coarse in quality, often dark in colour, and crudely ruled with staff lines. Most of the larger Bonn sheets have been damaged on the sides, which suggests that they suffered together in a single package.[15] The order of the manuscript appears to be largely arbitrary: occasionally there is a juxtaposition of different sheets referring to the same work (ff. 61, 62, 101, 102) or dating from the same period (ff. 123, 124, 125), but more frequently sheets that might be related in these ways are found widely separated. A systematic analysis of the quality and colour of the paper, staff-ruling characteristics, and watermarks reveals that as many as thirty-five different types of paper may be present, some of them represented by one or two sheets

xx

only. Table I (p. xxvi) lists and specifies these different papers. Table II (p. xxvii) presents an epitome of the 124 sheets of the miscellany grouped according to paper-types.

Rather than entering into detail at this point, it seems best to leave a discussion of the criteria of distinguishing the paper-types to an annotation to Table I (p. xxviii). As to Table II, a word of caution is necessary in regard to the interpretation of these data for establishing chronology. It may be probable, but it is not certain, that all sheets of a certain paper-type were originally used as a gathering; and in any case, grouping sheets according to physical criteria is not equivalent to associating the writing on those sheets. For Beethoven sometimes kept paper for long periods of time. This is especially clear with the paper designated as type 16f, the one type represented by a good number of sheets, 20 in all (2 gatherings of 2 bifolia each, 2 groups of 3 folios, 1 separate bifolium, and 4 single folios). The music that appears on these folios is known to date variously from 1793 or even 1792, 1794–5, and 1796. Therefore if we assume that the paper was all obtained at one time, we must conclude that Beethoven kept it for four years. A similar conclusion is suggested by a study of certain papers of other types.

Caution in the conduct of chronological arguments is also urged by some considerations about the fragmentary autographs in the miscellany: in particular, the fact that five of them consist of a single page which is the beginning of the composition. Beethoven usually began autographs not on the first, outer

[13] The gathering ff. 74–80 was all cut because its sheets, being in upright format, had to be mounted sideways, each from the top.

[14] See footnote 19, below.

[15] Other Bonn sheets which are damaged at the side, and which therefore may have formed part of the same package, are Berlin Staatsbibliothek, Beethoven Aut. 28 ff. 1, 2, 10, 15, 18, 19, Beethovenhaus MSS. 78 (burnt in 1960, but see facsimile in Ludwig Schiedermair, *Der junge Beethoven*, 3rd edn., Bonn, 1951, opp. p. 272) and 117, and Vienna, Gesellschaft der Musikfreunde 61.

page of a gathering but on the verso of the first sheet (see ff. 74, 104, 107); he must sometimes have torn off the front sheet of an autograph he was discarding just to have the blank recto page for sketching. Sketches and autograph, then, are not necessarily contemporary.

What has been said above about the sheets of paper-type 16f also militates against the possibility that the miscellany may preserve the torsos of any true sketchbooks. These twenty sheets, which would constitute the most likely candidate for such a torso, were used over a considerable span of time to sketch many different works. Half of the paper is devoted to actual sketches, the rest mainly to miscellaneous notations, and one sheet is the autograph of a completed composition (or the fragment of a larger autograph). Even if we suppose that the sheets were kept together in a portfolio, this portfolio was clearly not used in the way that regular sketchbooks were in a later period. In fact, there is no evidence that Beethoven used true sketchbooks at this early period, and there is some faint evidence that he did not. The most extensively sketched work in the miscellany is the rondo of the Piano Concerto No. 2 in B♭, Op. 19, which is also the most extensively sketched work that is known in the period prior to the earliest sketchbooks, those devoted to the String Quartets Op. 18, 1798–9. Rondo sketches appear on three bifolia of different paper characteristics (types 16f, 16l, 18). Taking into account all three movements of the concerto, sketches appear on seven different papers (types 12c, 16f, 16h, 16i, 16l, 16p, 18).

The facsimile published herewith has been prepared by off-set lithography at the size of the original pages. In view of the fact that only two pages use coloured ink or pencil, it was felt that a full colour process could be forgone, and that the loss of the range of colour of the paper and the inks used for the staff-ruling and the actual writing would not be too serious a disadvantage. The loss will perhaps grieve the general reader more than the scholar, who would not turn to a facsimile in any case for the purpose of studying ink and paper. For the purpose of reading the music, however, it is believed that the facsimile attains a very satisfactory standard. Where a confused or illegible situation exists in the facsimile, this will generally be found to reflect only too accurately a confused, illegible situation in the original source.

HISTORY OF THE MANUSCRIPT. A primary question that arises with a manuscript of this sort is when and by whom it was assembled. There is no documentary evidence on this point, nor any to be obtained from original bindings, since the material had to be rebound by the British Museum on acquisition, in 1875. Although the Museum has a considerable amount of correspondence with Kafka, none of it touches on the previous history of his manuscripts. However, it can be ascertained that during the 1860s and early 1870s the miscellany sheets were bound in one big book owned by the publishers and booksellers Artaria & Co. in Vienna. Thayer, in the second volume of *Ludwig van Beethoven's Leben*, 1872, speaks of a thick fascicle ('starkes Faszikel') at Artaria's in which miscellaneous sketches and musical fragments dating from the Bonn period to the end of the century were bound together, and from which he transcribed inscriptions that are now to be found on f. 59 of the miscellany.[16] On a copy that Nottebohm made of the 'Trinklied', WoO 109 (now ff. 107–8), he wrote 'aus dem dicken Skizzenbuch bei Artaria'.[17] Both Thayer and Nottebohm had consulted this

[16] Alexander Wheelock Thayer, *Ludwig van Beethoven's Leben*, ii (1872), 9.
[17] Kinsky-Halm, p. 572. Nottebohm also saw f. 126 (the fragmentary piano score of the scherzo of Op. 1 No. 2) when it was at Artaria: see Thayer's *Beethoven*, i, 2nd edn., ed. Hermann Deiters, 1901, p. 379, fn. 1.

thick book in connection with their catalogues of Beethoven's music, 1865 and 1868, and it clearly figures as the 'Grosses Notirungsbuch mit vielen Compositionen' entered in an old handwritten catalogue of Beethoven manuscripts (Beethoven Autograph MS. 47a in the Berlin Staatsbibliothek) which can be shown on internal evidence to refer to Artaria's holdings of around 1840.[18] The entry specifies the number of folios, 124, and there is a rough identification of some of the contents, added in the hand of Anton Schindler. Even the old front sheet presently bound with the miscellany can be traced to Artaria, where it was apparently transposed from another manuscript.[19]

Domenico Artaria had purchased heavily at the auction of Beethoven's *Nachlass* in November 1827. It is reasonably certain that the miscellany or the makings of the miscellany went directly from the auction to Artaria and from Artaria to Kafka. But it is not known whether Artaria or those in charge of the auction had any hand in selecting or arranging the material.

A fact of significance in this connection is the striking coherence of the collection. Of the 124 sheets, all but one or two (ff. 152 and 162) date from the Bonn years to 1797–8, and the exceptions are no more than a year or so later. It is hard to think of an individual in the early or middle nineteenth century who would have had both the knowledge of Beethoven's hand necessary to form such a specialized collection and also the opportunity (let alone the wish) to do so. One candidate might be Schindler, who was active with the *Nachlass*. But the simplest hypothesis is that while the collection may very well have been depleted over the years, it preserves part of a portfolio assembled before 1800 by Beethoven himself. The first true sketchbooks that are known date from 1798–9; this may indicate that the composer had recently settled on a method of work involving

xxii

sketchbooks rather than loose bifolia. We can imagine him sorting out his old sheets and keeping those that still interested him, including the remains of an even older portfolio, the famous portfolio that he had brought with him to Vienna from Bonn in 1792. In the next decades, he may occasionally have removed some pages—an old song to publish, an old sketch to consult—but doubtless there were long periods during which the collection was left undisturbed.

At some point, though, possibly after Beethoven's death, the portfolio was divided in two. The Berlin Staatsbibliothek contains a smaller miscellany (Beethoven Autograph MS. 28) of fifty-six sheets which are similar in date, physical character, and contents to those of the London book.[20] Indeed, some pages are demonstrably contiguous between the two collections: music beginning on f. 48^v of the Berlin miscellany continues directly on f. 141^r of the London, and music beginning on London f. 117^r continues on Berlin f. 20^r. The Berlin miscellany was owned by the Viennese pianist and professor Joseph Fischhof (1804–57), a well-known collector.

[18] Alexander W. Thayer, *Chronologisches Verzeichniss der Werke Ludwig van Beethoven's*, Berlin, 1865: No. 20—the autograph of the 'Trinklied', WoO 109, is said to be owned by Artaria (ff. 107-8); No. 43—Artaria owns sketches for 'Adelaide', Op. 46 (f. 44). *Thematisches Verzeichnis der im Druck erschienenen Werke von Ludwig van Beethoven*, 2nd edn., ed. Gustav Nottebohm, Leipzig, 1868: p. 177—Araria owns the autograph of 'Der Freie Mann', WoO 117 (f. 62). For information about Aut. 47a, and its analysis, the editor is greatly obliged to Mr. Douglas Johnson.

[19] This front sheet, with the cancelled title 'Notirungsbuch I 43', probably dates from the auction of Beethoven's *Nachlass* in 1827, but the pencilled note 'aus der 2te Messe/aus der C mol Sonate Op 111 C' (also cancelled) shows that the sheet did not originally come with the miscellany. Artaria bought auction lot 43 (described in the auction catalogue as 'Notirbuch und Notirungen': see *Neues Beethoven-Jahrbuch*, vi [1935], 76 and Thayer, *Chronologisches Verzeichniss*, p. 176) and he is known to have owned a sketchbook for the Mass and the C-minor Sonata (now Artaria 201 in the Berlin Staatsbibliothek: Schmidt, *Verzeichnis*, No. 14).

[20] Schmidt provides a preliminary list of contents (*Verzeichnis*, No. 31). Two of the sheets are from a later period. Information about this manuscript has been kindly put at the editor's disposal by Mr. Douglas Johnson.

Johann Nepomuk Kafka (1819–86) would have obtained his miscellany from Artaria after 1870. Like Fischhof, Kafka was a pianist and composer who lived in Vienna, a collector and something of an amateur dealer in manuscripts. At one time or another he owned the autographs of a number of Beethoven bagatelles, the Piano Sonatas in D, Op. 28, and C, Op. 53 ('Waldstein'), as well as various sketches, sketchbooks, and miscellanies.[21] A smaller manuscript known to have been in his possession is a bifolium now in the Beethovenhaus collection (MS. 114); this contains sketches and notations similar to many of those in the miscellany. This bifolium was also sold across the Channel, to a Professor William Cart of Edinburgh, who bequeathed it to the Beethovenhaus.[22]

The miscellany was first studied seriously by the pioneer and still recognized master of Beethoven sketch studies, Gustav Nottebohm. He first discussed material from the book in two short notices of 1869–71, and he published nine more articles dealing with it in 1875–6; six more appeared posthumously in 1887.[23] Nottebohm's primary interest in sketches was for the light they shed on the chronology of Beethoven's music, and he recognized in the miscellany an invaluable source of information about works of the early period, the period for which information is of course the scarcest. In point of fact, the accepted dates for some twenty works are derived from conclusions drawn by Nottebohm from the miscellany: Op. 1 Nos. 2 and 3, Op. 7, Op. 10 Nos. 2 and 3, Op. 11, 13, 14 No. 1, Op. 15, 16, 19, 37, 46, 49 Nos. 1 and 2, Op. 52 No. 3, Op. 71, WoO 6, 53, and 126. The typical Nottebohm *Aufsatz* treating a certain work presents some sketch transcriptions, often of late sketches which may be presumed to approach the time of the autograph, together with evidence bearing on the date of the sketches, such as inscriptions or other works on the same sheet. In one article Nottebohm went farther, illustrating the evolution of the Sonata in E, Op. 14 No. 1, by means of transcriptions of thirteen sketches for it on ff. 65 and 121–2. (These pages contain a total of twenty-eight such sonata sketches.) Nottebohm's laconic manner, which incidentally extended to a parsimony about exact manuscript references that is the despair of later scholars, should not be mistaken for desultoriness. He made some mistakes, but it is to be doubted whether many musical scholars have maintained so high a standard of accuracy and objectivity, and so sharp a sense of the relevant, in treating a similar mass of difficult material.

Once in London, the manuscript came to the attention of British scholars. A. J. Hipkins noticed in it the autograph of the Sonatina in C minor for Mandoline and Piano, WoO 43a (f. 87); this he published for the first time in *Grove* (1880, in the article 'Mandoline'). In 1892, the miscellany figured centrally in a long article by J. S. Shedlock, 'Beethoven's Sketch

[21] See Kinsky-Halm, pp. 69, 84, 125, 499, 502, 585. Kafka sold the British Museum another sketch miscellany, Add. 29997. A fine facsimile of the 'Waldstein' autograph was published in 1955 by the Beethovenhaus (*Veröffentlichungen des Beethovenhauses in Bonn. Neue Folge. 3. Reihe. Beethoven: Ausgewählte Handschriften in Faksimile-Ausgabe*, ii).

[22] Facs. and transcription in Schmitz, op. cit.

[23] *Beethoveniana*, 1872: No. 1, 'Ein Satz im Septett Op. 20 und die Sonate Op. 49 Nr. 2' and No. 17, 'Das Opferlied Op. 121ᵇ' (reprinted from *Allgemeine Musikalische Zeitung*, 3. Folge, iv [1869], 289–90, and vi [1871], 87–8); *Zweite Beethoveniana*, 1887: No. 3, 'Skizzen zu den Trios Op. 1 Nr. 2 und 3'; No. 4, 'Skizzen zu den Sonaten Op. 10'; No. 5, 'Das Rondo der Sonate Op. 13'; No. 6, 'Skizzen zur Sonate Op. 14 Nr. 1'; No. 7, 'Skizzen zu den letzten Sätzen der Quartette Op. 18 Nr. 1 und Nr. 6'; No. 8, 'Skizzen zum Clavierconcert in C dur (Op. 15)'; No. 9, 'Skizzen zum Clavierconcert in B dur (Op. 19)'; No. 26, 'Eine unvollendete Symphonie'; No. 37, 'Clavierspiel' (reprinted from *Musikalisches Wochenblatt*, vi [1875], 169, 577; vii [1876], 29; vi. 185 and 197, 633, 605, 605; vii. 17, 65 et seq.); No. 48, 'Der dritte Satz der Sonate in Es dur Op. 7'; No. 49, 'Einige Entwürfe zum Quintett Op. 16'; No. 50, 'Entwürfe zum Trio Op. 11 und zu unbekannten Stücken'; No. 57, 'Skizzen zur "Adelaide" und zu einigen andern Stücken'; No. 61, 'Frühe Compositionen'; and No. 63, 'Liegengebliebene Arbeiten'.

Books', which appeared serially in *The Musical Times*. Shedlock, who was the most eminent British Beethoven scholar of his time, presented 'not extracts from, but rather a supplement to Nottebohm'—and to some extent also a complement, for his interest was less in chronological aspects of the sketches than in musical aspects. It is necessary to say that Shedlock was less accurate than Nottebohm in reading Beethoven's hand, but he brought to light a great deal of extremely interesting material and discussed it with discernment. It is from Shedlock's article and the British Museum Catalogue entries made with his help that most scholars have taken their information about the manuscript. After it came to England, it rather characteristically fell outside the range of the heavy artillery of Beethoven research.[24]

The subsequent history of work with the miscellany is concerned less with sketches than with the identification and publication of the autographs, including both the *unica* and also the variant versions of known compositions. Several scholars have been active in this work: Fritz Stein, Jack Werner, A. E. F. Dickinson,[25] and especially Willy Hess, who over the years has occupied himself with many of the autographs and who is now (1970) incorporating them all into the supplements to the old Breitkopf & Härtel complete edition. In 1959, an entire sketch page from the miscellany (and a very difficult one) was published in transcription, in connection with an ingenious discovery made by Professor Joseph Schmidt-Görg, Director of the Beethovenhaus at Bonn.[26] An anecdote due to Wegeler tells how young Beethoven, as assistant organist of the Electoral Chapel at Bonn, threw the singers out by his unorthodox harmonizations of the Lamentations of Jeremiah during Holy Week. Schmidt-Görg saw that f. 96[r] bears numerous settings of the plainchant for the Lamentations, some of them startling

indeed, and also the names of two singers identifiable from Bonn Chapel records.

*   *   *

One other miscellany of early Beethoven autograph material is known, the Berlin manuscript Beethoven Autograph 28. As has been mentioned above, this consists of some fifty-six sheets from the same period as the London book; almost certainly these sheets and the 124 London sheets once formed part of a single portfolio. Nottebohm drew on the Berlin miscellany for his articles dealing with Beethoven's early music, and it has been examined in detail for the purposes of the present edition. The first true sketchbooks that have survived are a pair from the years 1798–9, devoted principally to the String Quartets Op. 18 (Berlin, Grasnick 1 and 2). For the rest, early sketch and other autograph material is to be found on a comparatively small number of single sheets and bifolia located in the various Beethoven archives or in private collections.

For studies of Beethoven's late Bonn and early Vienna periods, then, the London miscellany occupies a centrally important

[24] One person who examined the manuscript at first hand, in an attempt to verify Nottebohm's hypotheses about chronology, was Theodor Müller-Reuter, author of the *Lexikon der deutschen Konzertliteratur*. The supplementary volume (Leipzig, 1921) includes transcriptions of a few sketches and inscriptions from the miscellany.

[25] See Fritz Stein, 'Eine unbekannte Jugendsymphonie Beethoven's?', *Sammelbände der internationalen Musikgesellschaft*, xiii (1912) [includes Hess 298, pp. 131–2]; *Duett mit zwei obligaten Augengläsern* [WoO 32], Peters, Leipzig, 1912. Karl Haas, *Minuetto, Second Movement of the Sonata 'Duett mit zwei obligaten Augengläsern'* [ibid.], Peters, Frankfurt and London, 1952. A. E. F. Dickinson, 'Beethoven's Early Fugal Style', *Musical Times*, xcvi (1955) [includes Hess 64, pp. 78–9]. Jack Werner, *Fugue in C* [ibid.], J. Williams, London, 1956; *Allegretto in E flat* [Hess 48], Elkin, London, 1955; *The Beethoven Sketchbooks*, Chappell, London, 6 vols., 1961–2 (a bizarre edition of several dozen items from the miscellany arranged very freely as children's piano pieces).

[26] Joseph Schmidt-Görg, 'Ein neuer Fund in den Skizzenbüchern Beethovens: die Lamentationen des Propheten Jeremias', *Beethoven-Jahrbuch*, iii (1959), 107–11.

place. Although this source has been well known for nearly a century, information about it has been scattered and hard to come by, incomplete, and not always accurate, and the extent of its contents cannot be said to have been fully appreciated. Its publication by the British Museum in co-operation with the Royal Musical Association, on the occasion of the bicentennial of the composer's birth, contributes a fresh body of evidence towards an understanding of Beethoven's formative period.

JOSEPH KERMAN

TABLE I. TABLE OF PAPER-TYPES

TYPE	PAPER CHARACTERISTICS		STAFF-RULING	Total span	Single staff	Ruling-ink	WATERMARK Left sheet	Right sheet
8	stiff, light brown	25 × 30½ cm.	8, one at a time (cf. 10b)[1]	186 mm.	10 mm.	dark brown	AMICITIAE	MUSIS
10a	fine grain, off-white	22½ × 31	10, one at a time	196	10	light brown	–	
b	light brown	24½ × 30	10, one at a time (cf. 8)[1]	198	9½	dark brown	–	
c	stiff, grey	24 × 31½-32	10 at a time(?)	185	9½	brown	crest/WVV(?)	6(?) letters
d	pliable, off-white	24 × 33	10 at a time	183-4	8½	grey	three moons	crown/CAF(?)
e	white	23 × 31½	10 at a time	188	8½	light grey	three moons	[bow/MA]
12a	grey	21 × 25½	12 similar ruling,	182	7½	light brown	H BLUM	fleur de lys
b	light beige	21 × 26½	12 12 at a time	181-2	7½	light brown	crown/shield	
c	white	23 × 32	12 at a time	187-8	7½	light grey	three moons	FC (or G)
d	off-white	24 × 31	12 at a time	189	8½	brown	central fleur de lys	
e	off-white	23 × 33	12 at a time	188-9	8½	grey-brown	three moons	
15a	thin, light brown	21½ × 35	15 at a time	186	6	light brown	–	–
b	stiff, light brown	26 × 36	15, one at a time	240	9½	dark brown	shield, bent	–
16a	beige	33-34 × 21	16 similar ruling, two at	280-5	8½[2]	brown	IA VA(?)	arms of Amsterdam
b	beige	32 × 20	16 a time; upright format	283	8½[2]	brown	small crest	
c	light brown	23-24 × 39	16, eight at a time	204-7	7	grey-brown	NH	fleur de lys
d	smooth, light brown	24 × 36	16 at a time	201-8	6	light brown	unicorn/C A BACH	
e	stiff, light brown	22½-24½ × 30-31½	16 at a time	208-9	7½	light brown	W or VV(?)	
f	off-white	23 × 32½	16 at a time, continuous[3]	192-4	6½-7	grey-brown	moons/REAL	bow/AZ or AΣ
g	smooth, off-white	23 × 31½	16 at a time	190	6½	light grey	A[/HF/REAL]	crest with stars
h	white	23 × 32½	NOTE: on the remaining 16-staff paper-types, the rulings (all 16 at a time) are quite similar and often hard to distinguish.	190	6½	dark grey	–	
i	off-white	22½ × 32		190-1	6½	dark grey	three moons	crown/A/GF/c
j	smooth, white	23 × 32		190	7	light grey	three moons	crown
k	white	23 × 32		192	7	brown	three moons	GFA (large)
l	off-white	22½ × 31½		193	6½	grey-brown	three moons	GFA (small)
m	stiff, off-white	23 × 30½		193	7	tan	three moons	
n	stiff, off-white	23 × 31½		192	7	tan	moons/REAL	
o	off-white	23½ × 31½		191	7	grey	three moons	
p	pliable, off-white	23 × 32		190	6½	grey	three moons	PS
q	off-white	22½ × 31		192	6½	light grey	three moons	shield
r	stiff, off-white	23 × 32		189	6½	grey-brown	moons/REAL	GAF
s	stiff, off-white	23 × 31		192	7	black-brown	eagle/CFA(?)	three moons
t	white	23 × 32½		192-3	7	light grey	crown/GF	three moons
18	off-white	23 × 31½	18 at a time	182-3	6	grey-brown	three moons	shield with W

[1] On these papers margins were drawn in light pencil to guide the staff-ruling, and the ruling pen was probably the same.

[2] The second staff is slightly smaller.

[3] i.e. the staffs were ruled all the way across the fold in the centre of the bifolia.

TABLE II. FOLIOS GROUPED ACCORDING TO PAPER-TYPES

Folios are listed on the same line when they are known or thought to have belonged originally in a single gathering. Bifolia are indicated by hyphens or brackets between the folio numbers.

TYPE	FOLIOS	WORKS COPIED OR SKETCHED, WITH DATES
Bonn Papers		
10a	130	WoO 90 (c. 1790), Duo for Violin and Violoncello
12a	107–8	WoO 109 (c. 1790)
12b	153	WoO 117 (1791–2), Hess 58
	124	WoO 13, Composition in G for Orchestra: Oboe Part, Allemandes and Contredanses
15a	88	WoO 88 (October 1790)
16a	74 75 76 77 78 79 80	Hess 13 (c. 1786–7), WoO 6, 92, Cadenza in G
16b	70	Hess 298 (c. 1788–9)
16c	123 125	WoO 65 (1790)
	129	Hess 48
	96	Lamentations (1790–2)
16d	61	WoO 117 (Hess 146: 1791–2)
16e	100	WoO 67 (1791–2), Op. 75 No. 3, Composition (cantata?) in B♭
	50	WoO 14
	154	WoO 14, Piano Concerto in A
Vienna Papers		
8	84–5	Quartet(?) in G for Wind Instruments and Piano
10b	73	WoO 43a, 44b (1796)
10c	48 49	Op. 16 (1796–7)
	81–2 83	Op. 5 Nos. 1 and 2 (1796), 16, 37, WoO 78(?), Symphony Slow Movement in E
	142	Op. 5 No. 1 (1796)
10d	58 59	Op. 7, WoO 71 (1796–7), Op. 10 No. 3, Symphony in C
	101	Op. 10 No. 2 (1796–8), Sonata Movement in C minor (i)
10e	117	Sonata Movement in C minor (ii)
12c	131 132–3 134	Op. 19 (1795), Rondo in A, Song in E♭
12d	109 110–11 155 156 157	Op. 6 (1796–7), Canon 'Meine Herren' Op. 10 No. 3 (1796–8), WoO 11 (1798), Op. 37
12e	102 103	Op. 8, 10 No. 3, 71, WoO 53 (1796–7), Canon in A
	112	
15b¹	119	Op. 5 Nos. 1 and 2 (1796), 16, WoO 32
16f	150 151	Hess 12 (1793 or 1792), Sonata Movement in C (ii)
	116	Op. 1 Nos. 2 and 3 (1794–5), WoO 118 (1795)
	140 160–1 141	Op. 52 No. 3 (1795?), Song in C (ii), Composition (bagatelle?) in C for Piano
	39 40–1 42	Song in G (i), Composition (rondo?) in C for Piano
	45	Op. 19 (1795)
	97–8 99	Op. 19 (1795), 15, Minuet in F for Orchestra
	87	WoO 43a (1796)
	104 105 106	Op. 49 No. 2, 65, 71, WoO 43b, 44a (1796)
	55	
16g	120	Op. 52 No. 2 (1793?)
	68–9 86	Op. 1 Nos. 2 and 3 (1794–5), WoO 126
16h	139	Op. 1 No. 3 (1793?)
	46–7	Op. 19 (1795), Song in C (i), WoO 13
	149	Sonata Movement in E♭ (1797–8), Sonata Movement in C (i), Song in C (iii)
16i	126 127 128	Op. 1 No. 2, 19 (1795), WoO 14, Symphony in C
	56–7	Symphony in C
	72	WoO 8 (November 1795), Op. 15
	158 159	Hess 64 (1795), WoO 44a (1796), Symphony in C, Variations on 'Là ci darem la mano' (cello)
16j	114 115	Composition in D for Orchestra (1795?)
16k	135 136–7 138	WoO 32 (1796–7), Op. 15
	43	Song in G (ii) (1797–8)
16l	147–8	Op. 19 (1795)
16m	44	Op. 46 (1795)
16n	113	Op. 15 (1795–8)
16o	71	Op. 66 (before 1798), Symphony in C
16p	89 90 91–2 93 94 95	Op. 19 (1795), Composition (fantasia?) in D major/minor for Piano
	51 52 53 54	Op. 52 No. 3 (1795?), Song in G (iii), Composition (rondo?) in D for Piano
16q	60 62	WoO 117, 119 (1795), Study(?) in A♭ for Piano
16r	143 144–5 146	Op. 9 No. 1, 11 (1797–8), Sonata Movement in C minor (i)
	118	
16s	66 67	Op. 9 No. 1, 13, 49 No. 1 (1797–8), Song in G (ii)
	63	
16t	152 162	Op. 18 No. 5 (1799)
18	64–5	Op. 19 (1795), 14 No. 1, Composition in D for Orchestra
	121–2	Op. 14 No. 1

¹ In quality and staff-ruling, this paper resembles neither the typical Bonn nor the Vienna papers. It may be conjectured that Beethoven obtained it on his travels in 1796; other sheets of the same type (Berlin Beethoven Aut. 28ff. 9, 13–14, 16–17) also contain material from 1796–7.

ANNOTATIONS TO TABLE I, p. xxvi. The size of the paper is given to the nearest half-centimetre, since within any paper-type the dimensions vary within a half-centimetre or more, even when there has been no cropping. Dimensions are given in millimetres for the total staff span, i.e. the distance from the top of the first staff to the bottom of the last, and are estimated to the nearest half-millimetre for the individual staff width.

Paper-types can be distinguished by physical characteristics of the paper (size, colour, and texture), the staff-ruling, and the watermarks, though none of these criteria can always be applied with certainty. With the colour of the paper and ruling-ink, the effects of ageing and fading are hard to estimate. With watermarks, the fact that there are usually so few sheets of any one paper-type introduces a special limitation. Since watermarks were generally centred on the left- and right-hand sides of the large paper sheets which were cut in two laterally to make bifolia, the watermarks tended to be cut in two also; therefore if the full watermark is to be viewed two adjoining bifolia (or four sheets) have to be present, which is seldom the case with this manuscript. There may be enough of a watermark visible to match it with other marks, but not enough to be sure that the attempted description is complete.

Paper used for music in Vienna in the eighteenth century was mostly Lombard in origin. The common left-hand watermark was three crescent moons of descending sizes, a mark indicative of paper quality (*tre lune* paper), sometimes over the word 'REAL' (royal size). With the numerous single sheets bearing such moons (or, usually, cut moons), an attempt has been made to group or distinguish them according to the size of the design and its position in relation to the vertical chain lines. It should be remembered that moulds often came in pairs with similar but not quite identical watermarks. See Jan LaRue, 'Watermarks and Musicology', *Acta Musicologica*, xxxiii (1961), 120–46.

Few of the watermarks found in the manuscript can be exactly identified —let alone dated—on the basis of the various published watermark lists, but many similarities can be pointed out: see the Notes on Watermarks, below.

Paper-types can also be distinguished by the characteristics of their staff-ruling. This is a promising but so far little developed line of investigation: see Owen Jander, 'Staff-liner Identification, a Technique for the Age of Microfilm', *Journal of the American Musicological Society*, xx (1967), 112–16. It is known that eighteenth-century copyists and composers used a five-nib pen (*Rastral*) to draw the staffs, perhaps with the aid of a template: see paper-types 8, 10c, 15b. But in Beethoven's time it was more usual to obtain paper lined (not printed) by a device which did all the staffs at once. In England a machine for this purpose was patented in 1770 (Berry and Poole, *Annals of Printing*, p. 180). Such lined papers sometimes match over the entire span of 10, 12, 16, or 18 staffs as to the size of the staffs, the uneven distances between them, anomalies in the inking and spacing of the lines, horizontal irregularities at the beginning of the lines, etc.: see for example sheets of paper-type 12e. Without a clearer picture than is available of the actual process used, however, it is hard to judge tolerances, and it may be that certain paper-types with slightly different ruling characteristics should be amalgamated. Cleaning of the pens might have caused some realignment, and this might account for the 16-staff papers with ruling characteristics that are similar but not quite identical.

By and large a one-to-one correspondence is observed between papers with distinct watermarks and distinct staff-ruling characteristics. However, Beethoven could have been sold batches of paper consisting of sheets with different watermarks all ruled at the same time: see paper-types 12a and 12b.

NOTES ON WATERMARKS (references: Paper Publications Society, i: Heawood, *Watermarks*; vii: Tschudin, *Ancient Paper-Mills of Basle*; viii: Eineder, *Paper-Mills of the Austro-Hungarian Empire*; xi: Tromonin, *Watermark Album*; H. Robbins Landon, *The Symphonies of Haydn*, App. I; *Neue Mozart-Ausgabe* (NMA), *kritische Berichte* to ser. x, 28, i, vols. 2 and 3; Joseph Schmidt-Görg, *Katalog der Handschriften des Beethoven-Hauses und Beethoven-Archivs Bonn*.)

8. The watermark, illegible on the London sheets, is supplied from Berlin Gr. 25, the autograph of the Adagio in E♭ for Mandoline and Piano, WoO 43b, 1796 (information kindly provided by Mr. Douglas Johnson).

10d. CAF for Cartiera (paper-mill) Andreoli Fratelli of Toscolano (Eineder, p. 175); the same crown appears in Eineder 485. GAF papers are also associated with this mill: see 16i, 16k, 16l, 16r, 16s, 16t. A crown with GFA is the most common watermark in the sketchbook of 1800 transcribed by Mikulicz (see p. 5 of his edition).

10e. The right-hand watermark is supplied from Berlin Aut. 28, ff. 20, 32, 43. AM stands for Andreas Maffizzoli of Toscolano (Eineder 442, etc.; *NMA* x/28/i/2, wm. 9). The bow watermark also appears on paper 16f.

12a. Hieronymus Blum was a paper-maker in Basle from 1756 to 1788. His watermarks occasionally include fleurs de lys; cf. Tschudin 407, 352.

12b. Probably a fleur de lys in the shield below the crown, where the watermark is cut: cf. Tschudin 407 (Blum) and many others.

12c. These letters occur in Landon 29.

15b. The absence of a countermark is attested by bifolia of this paper in Berlin Aut. 28, ff. 13–14 and 16–17.

16a. Arms of Amsterdam occur in Heawood 343–437, mostly English and Dutch sources.

16c. NH could stand for Niklaus Heusler, a Basle paper-maker from 1788 to 1804: see Tschudin 327, 397, etc.

16f. Schmidt-Görg i, k, l, on the autograph of the Rondino for Wind Instruments, WoO 25 (1792? For a facsimile showing the characteristic continuous staff lines ruled across the fold of the bifolium, see Unger, *Beethovens Handschrift*, Tafel VI). Tromonin 719 (1780); cf. Landon 62. The bow watermark also appears on paper 10e.

16g. Only the 'A' appears, but the full watermark is shown in the facsimile edn. of Mozart's Requiem, 1791, ed. A. Schnerich, p. 14. The crest (but with three moons as countermark) also appears in the autograph of Beethoven's Op. 3 at the Library of Congress. Other versions of this crest in Eineder 371 (1788), Heawood 824 (1784).

16i. Cf. Eineder 485.

16j. Cf. *NMA*, x/28/i/3, wm. 9.

16l. Cf. *NMA*, x/28/i/2, wm. 8.

16p. These letters occur in Eineder 390, 871, Landon 24, *NMA*, x/28/i/2, wm. 11.

16q. Cf. *NMA*, x/28/i/3, wm. 3.

16s. Cf. Eineder 520, Heawood 1262–3, Tromonin 720.

16t. Cf. Eineder 485, 434.

INVENTORY

THIS summary inventory lists the works copied or sketched on the various folios, including known works by Beethoven, unfinished works that are sketched at some length, and works by other composers. No reference is made to unidentified smaller sketches and miscellaneous notations which appear on the majority of the pages. The italic numbers refer to pages in the transcription, Volume II.

INDEX OF WORKS COPIED OR SKETCHED

Folio numbers are printed in bold type when the folios contain autographs, in ordinary
type when they contain sketches

xxxix

Notirungsbuch

N J

43

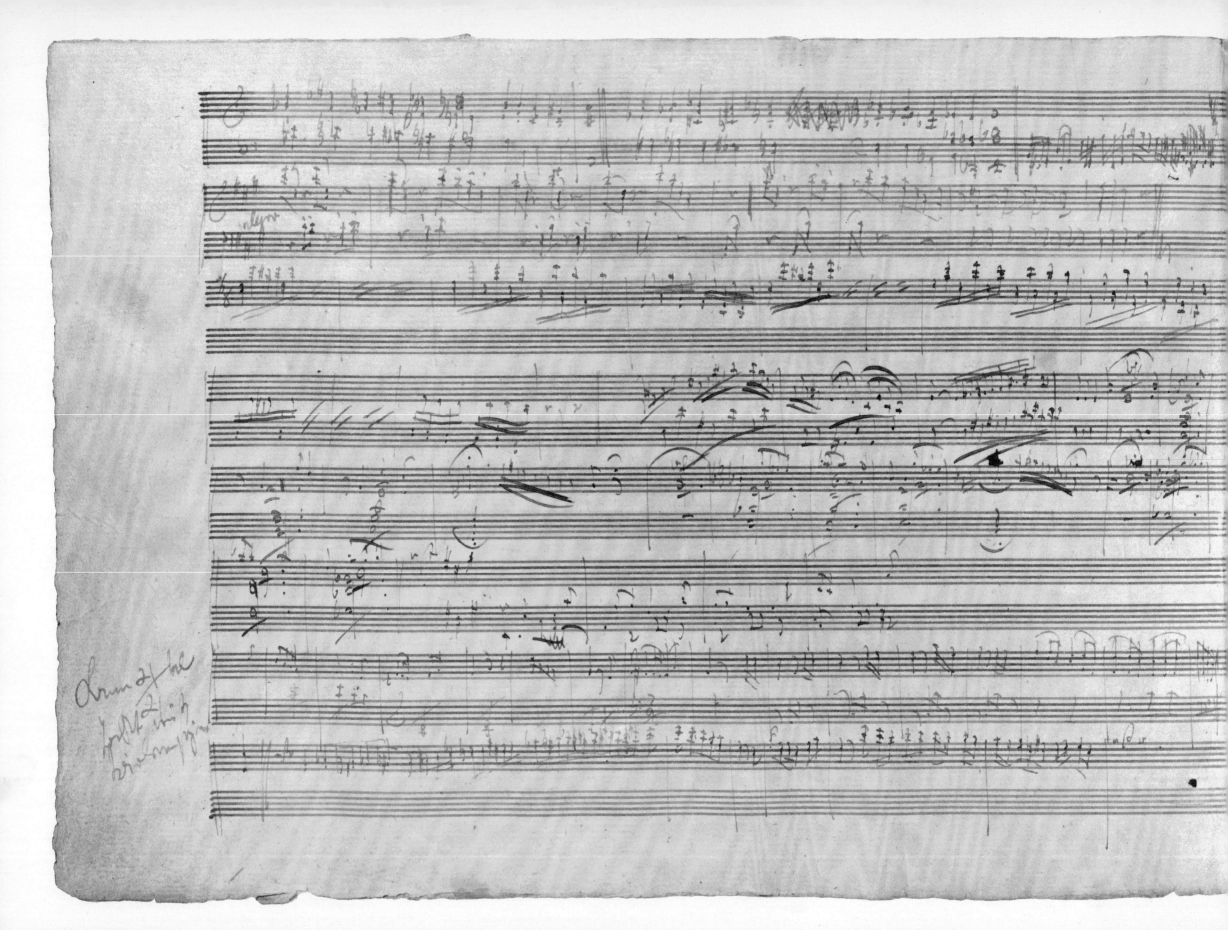

f. 40v

f. 41v

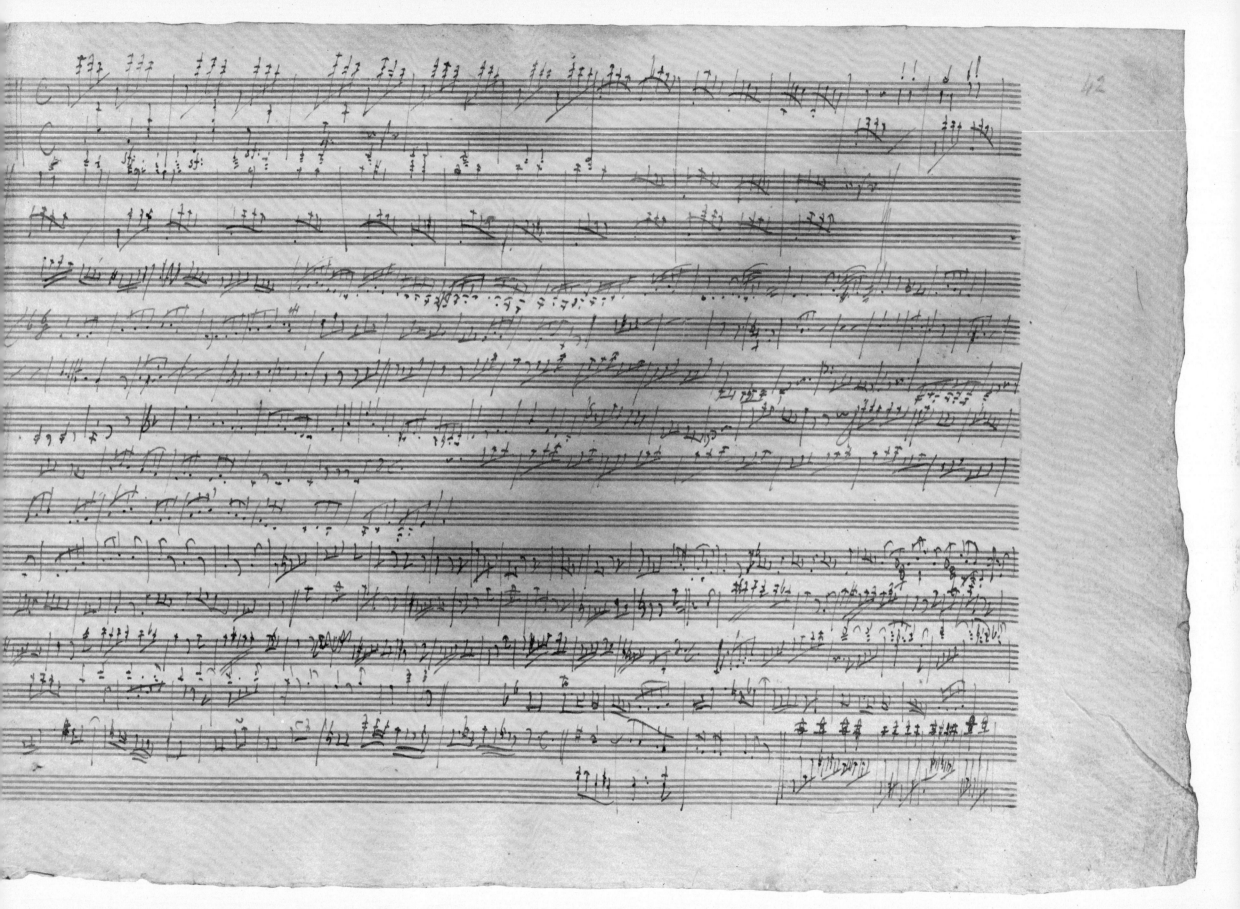

f. 42v

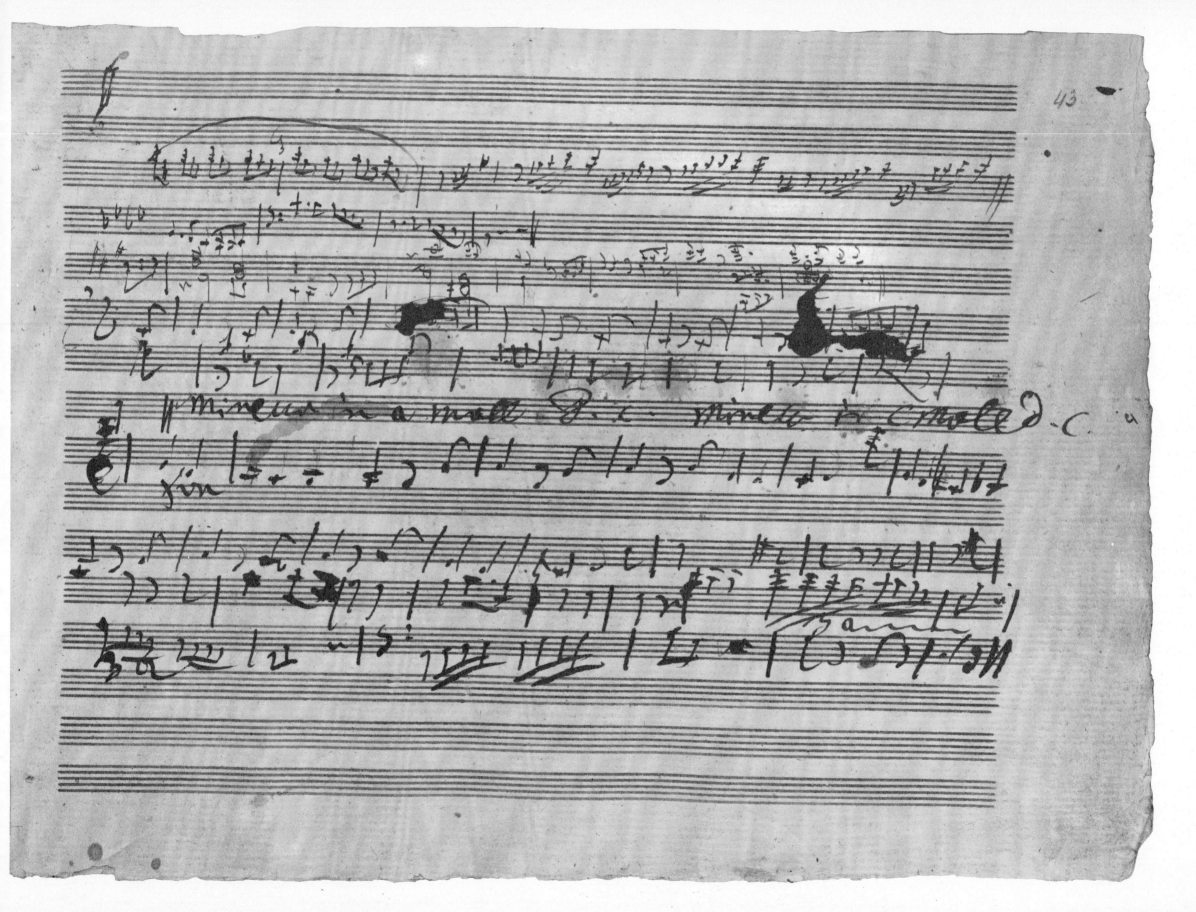

f. 44v

f. 45v

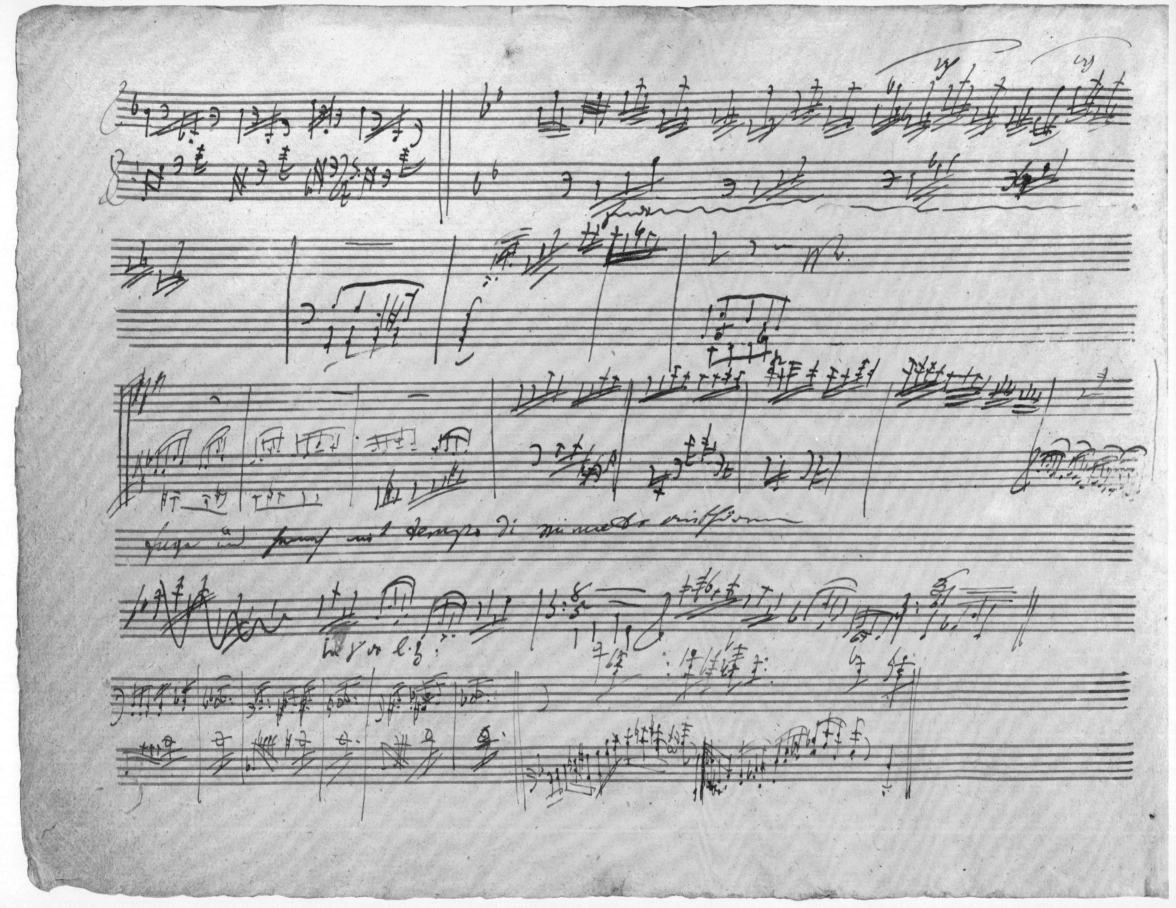

f. 49v

f. 51v

53

f. 53r

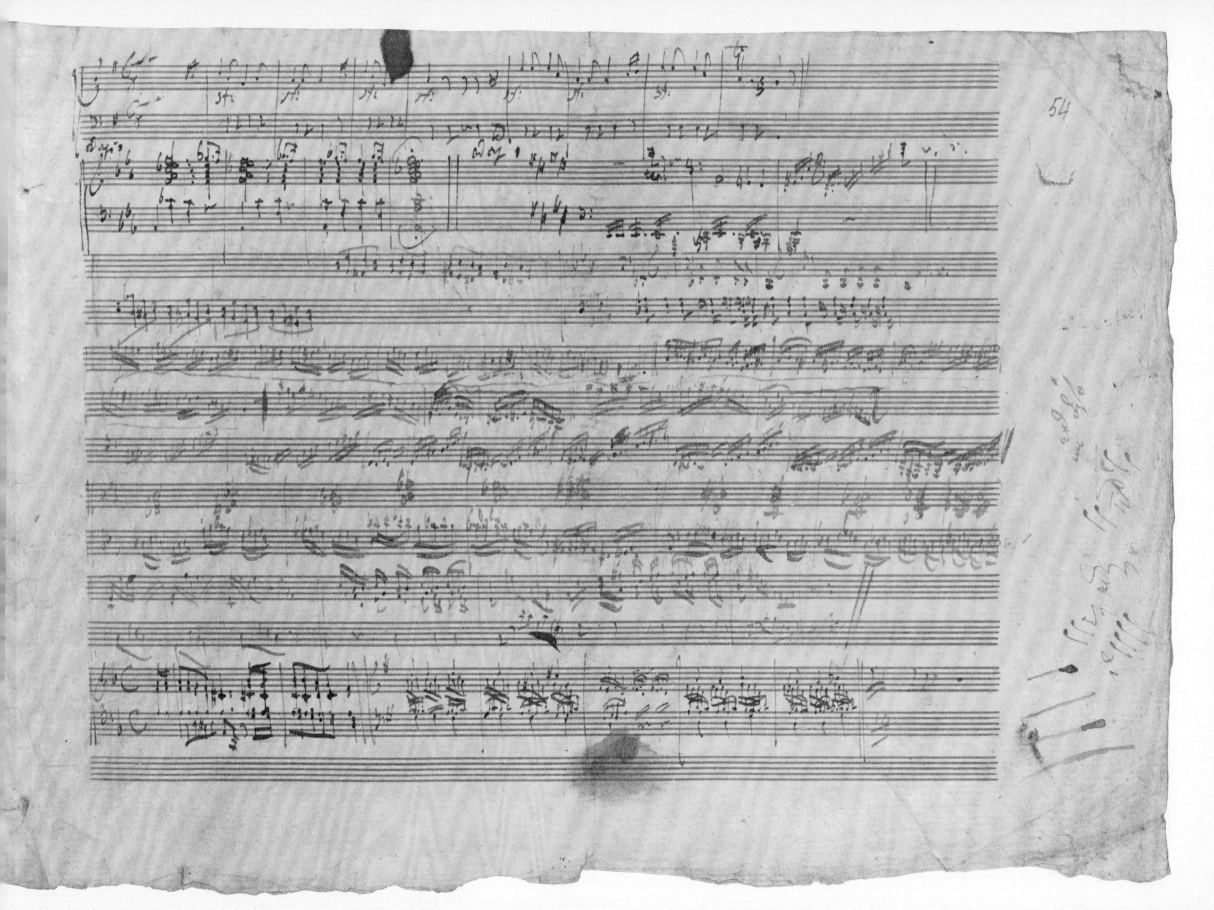

f. 55v

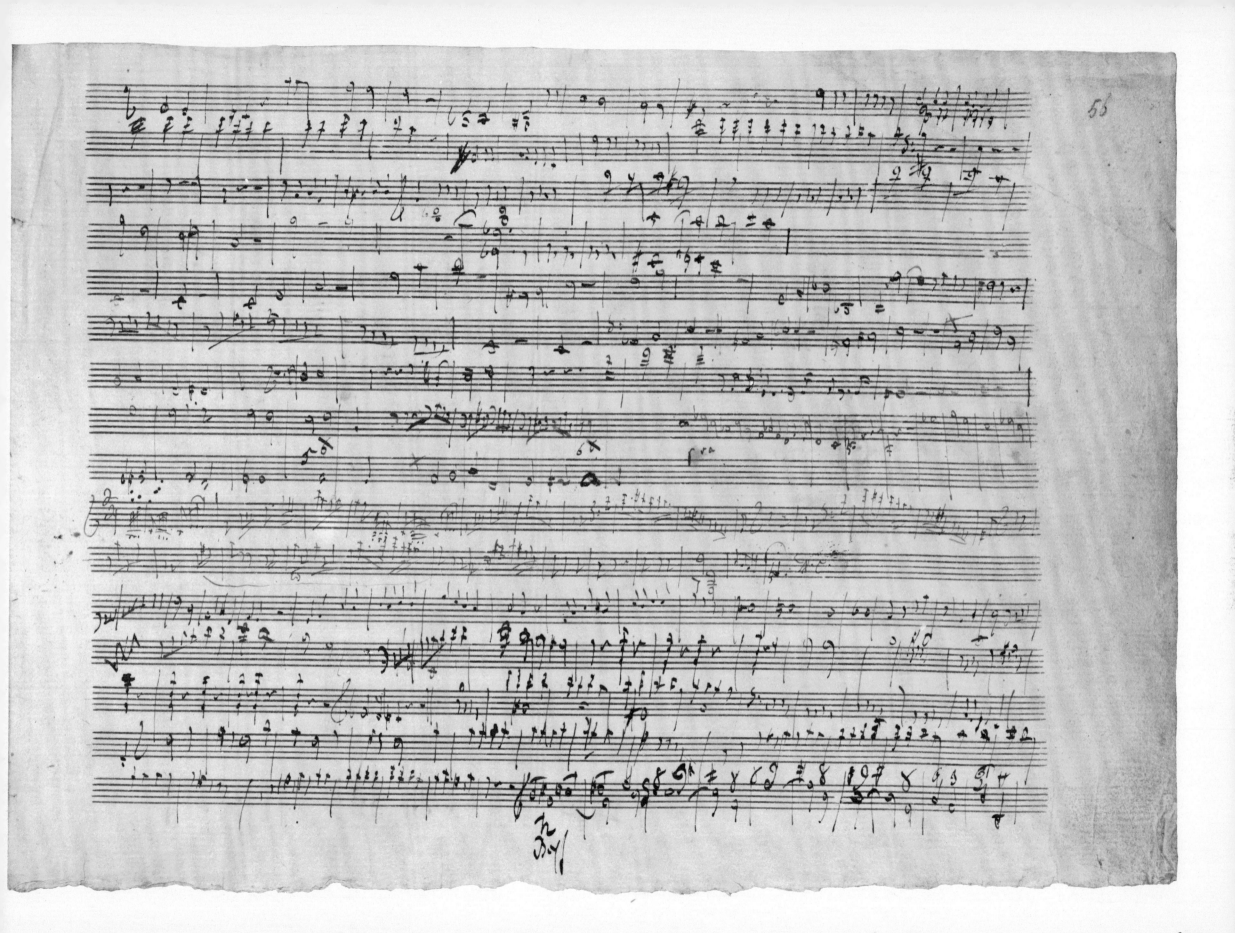

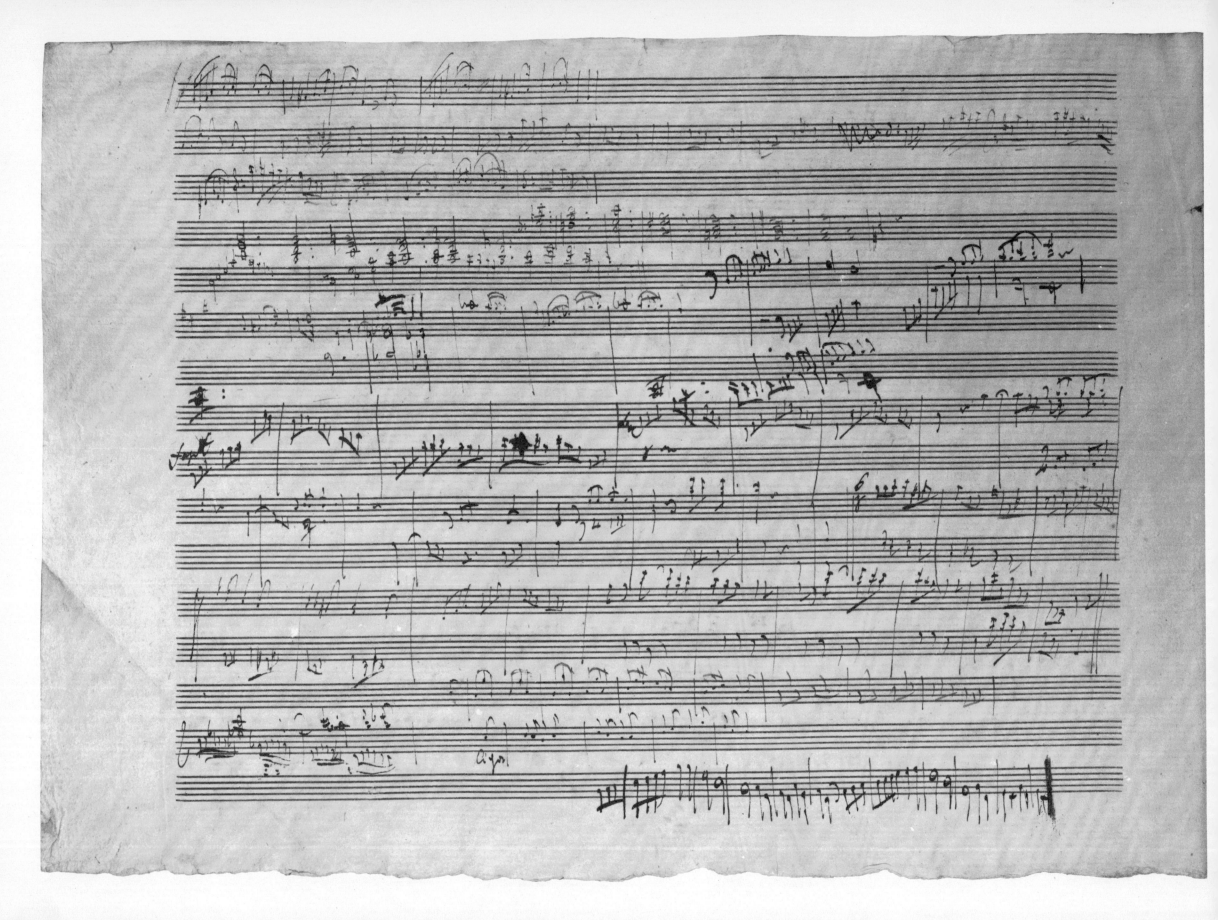

f. 56v

57

f. 57r

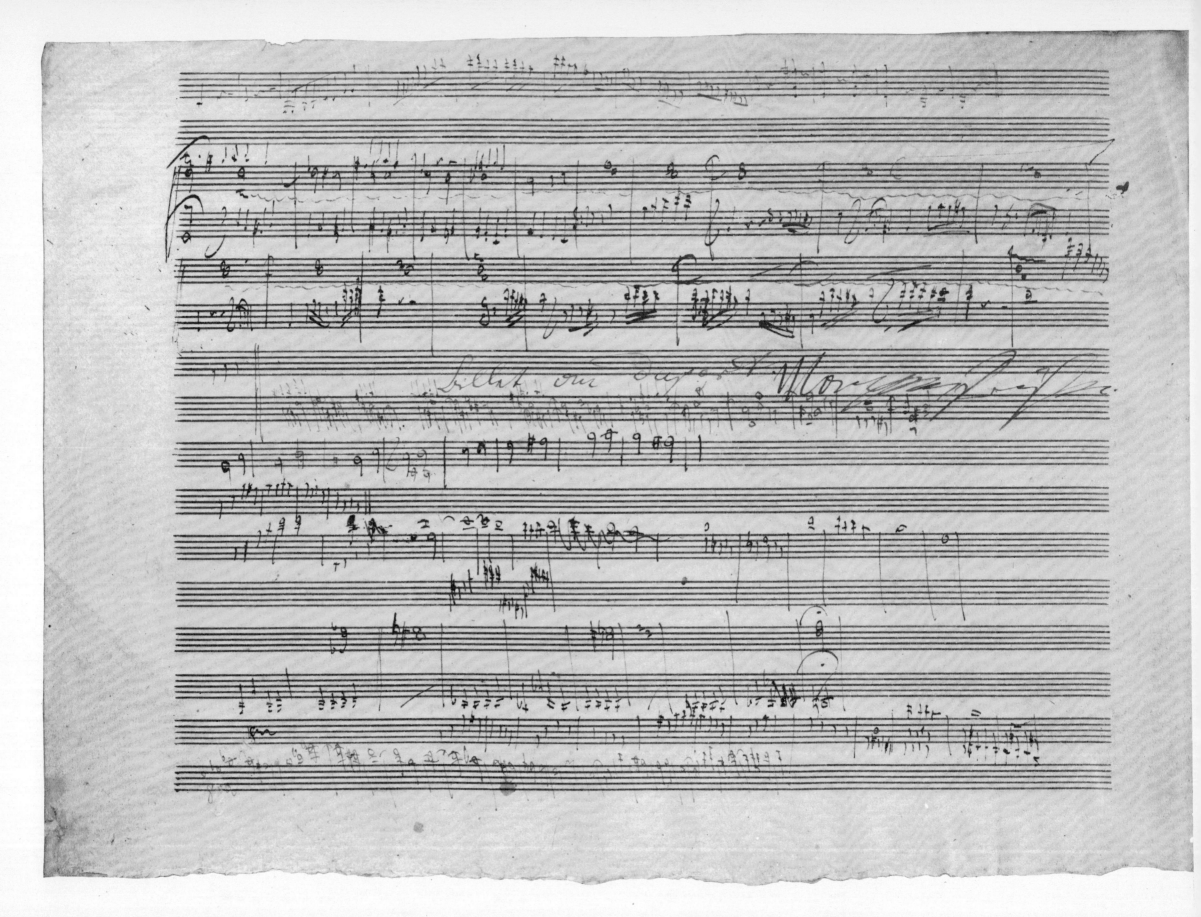

f. 57v

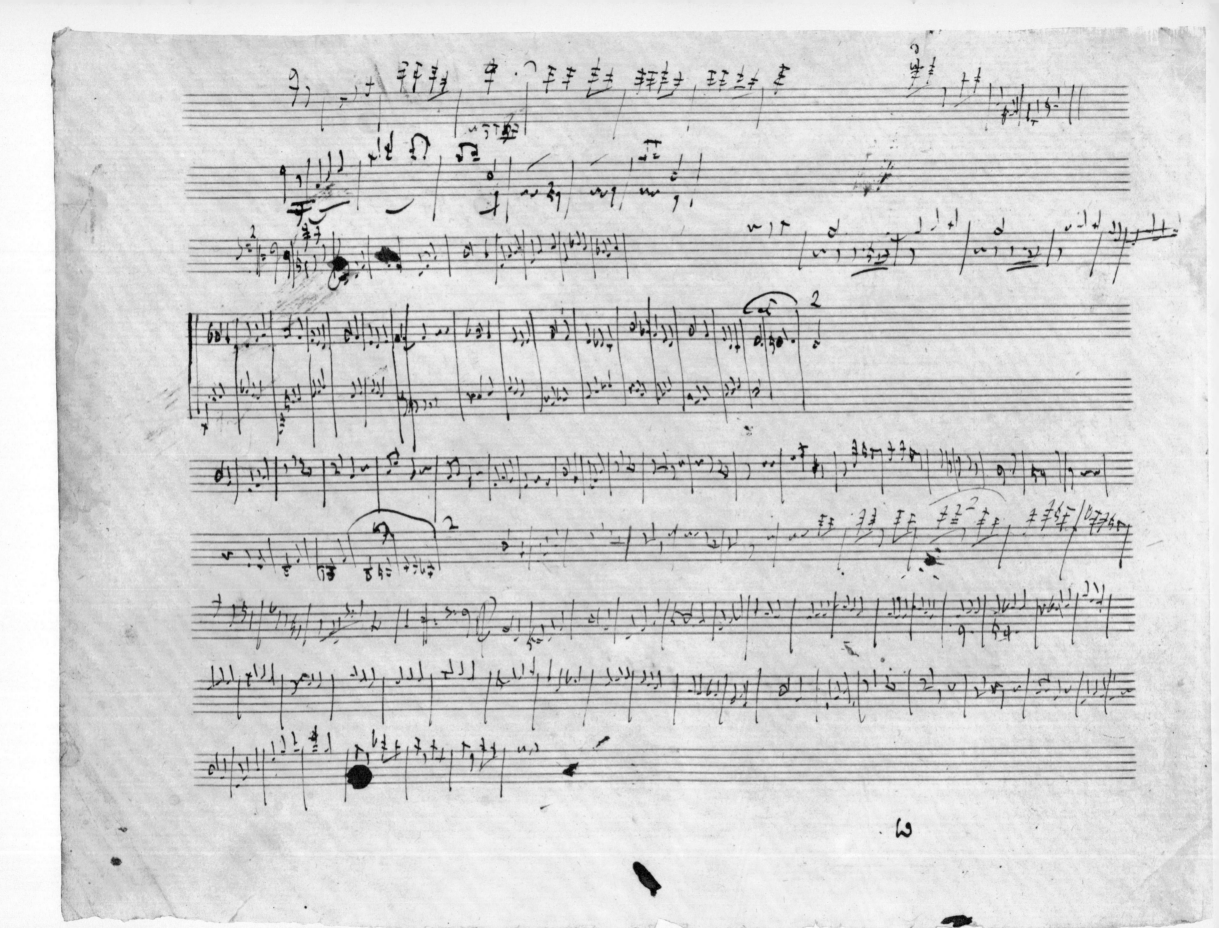

f. 58v

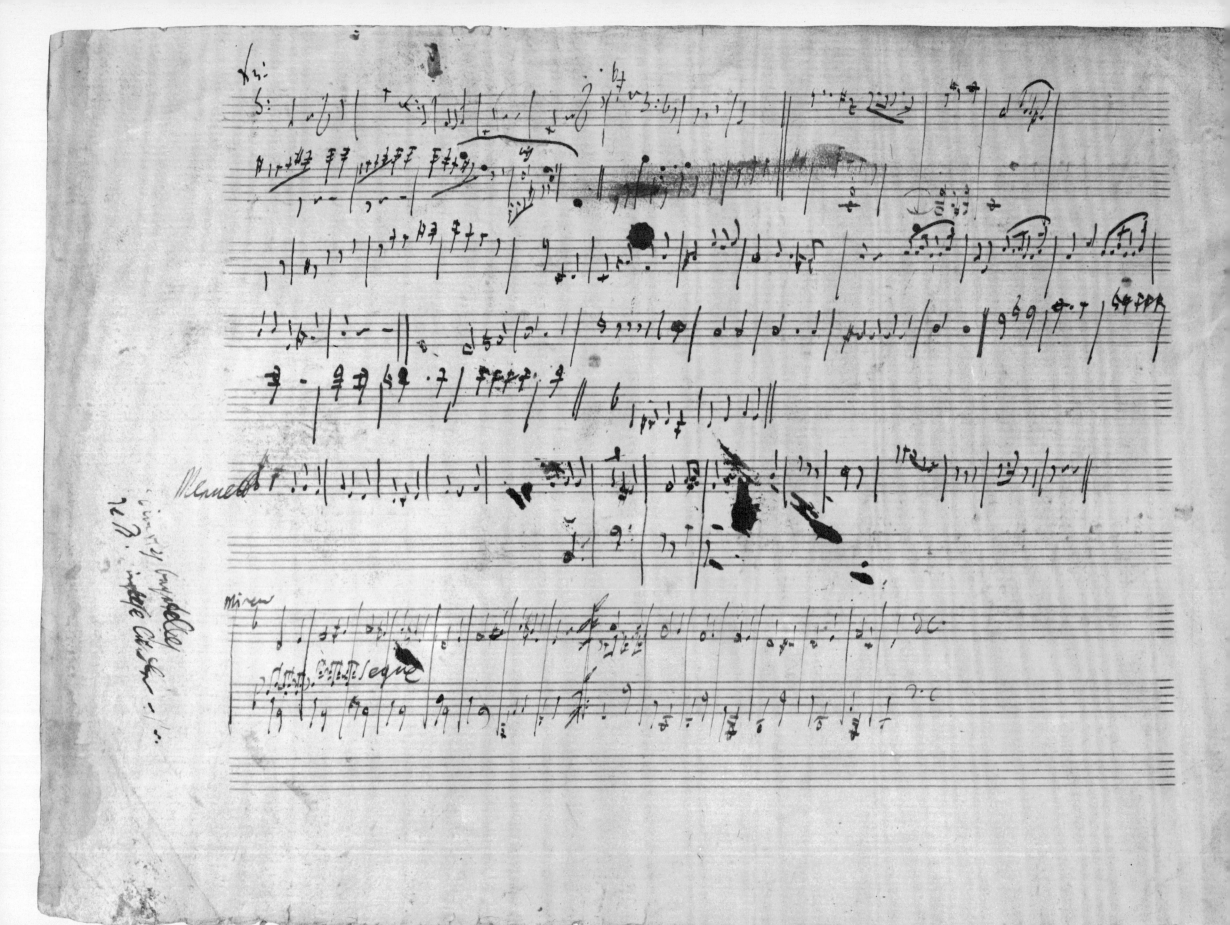

f. 59v

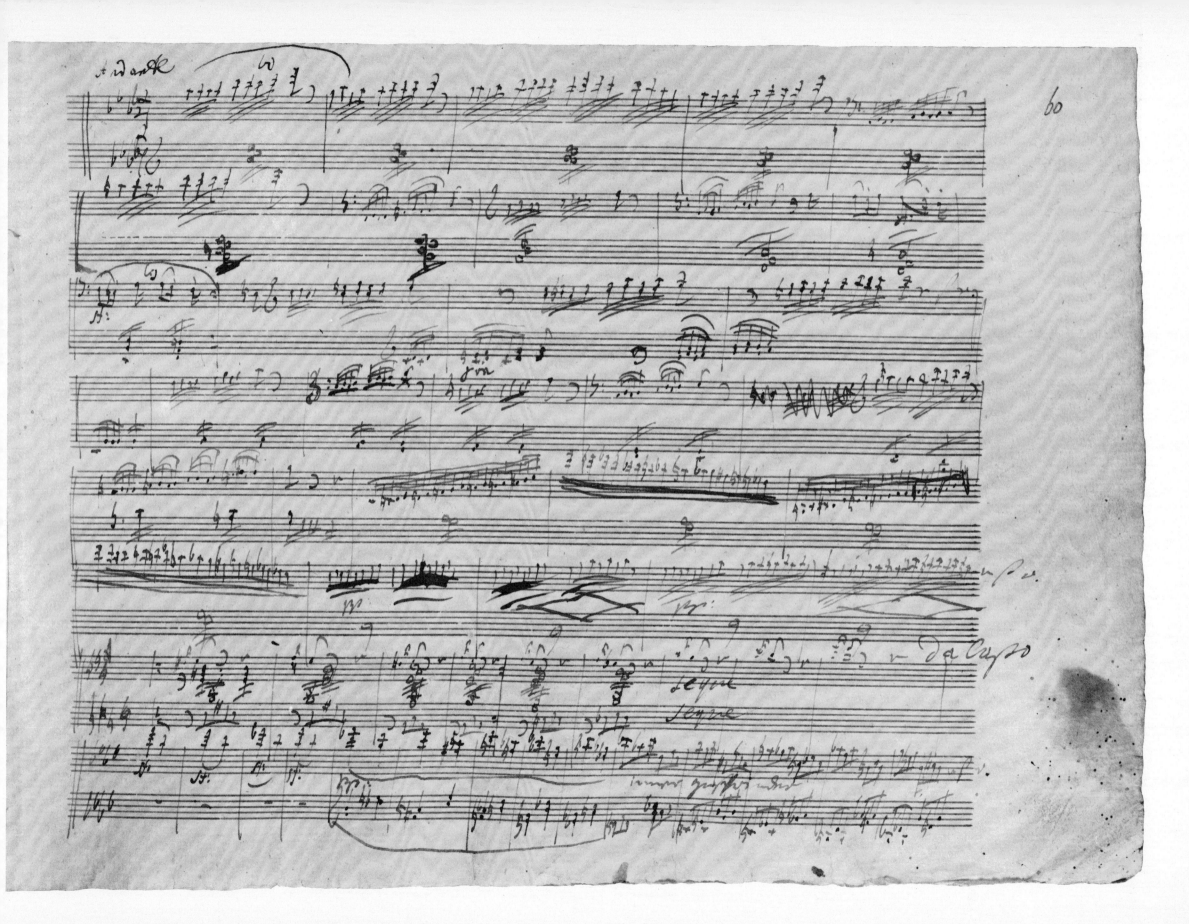

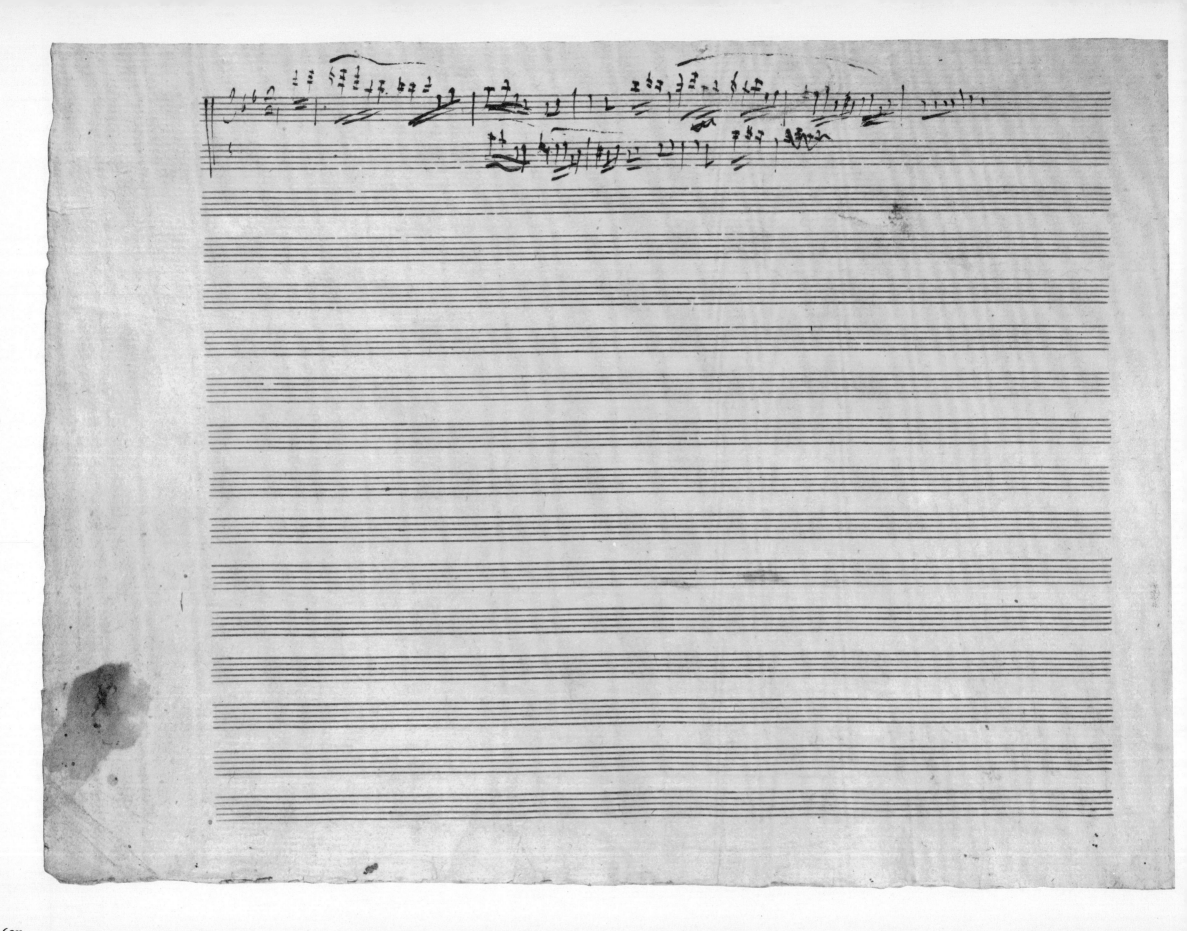

f. 6ov

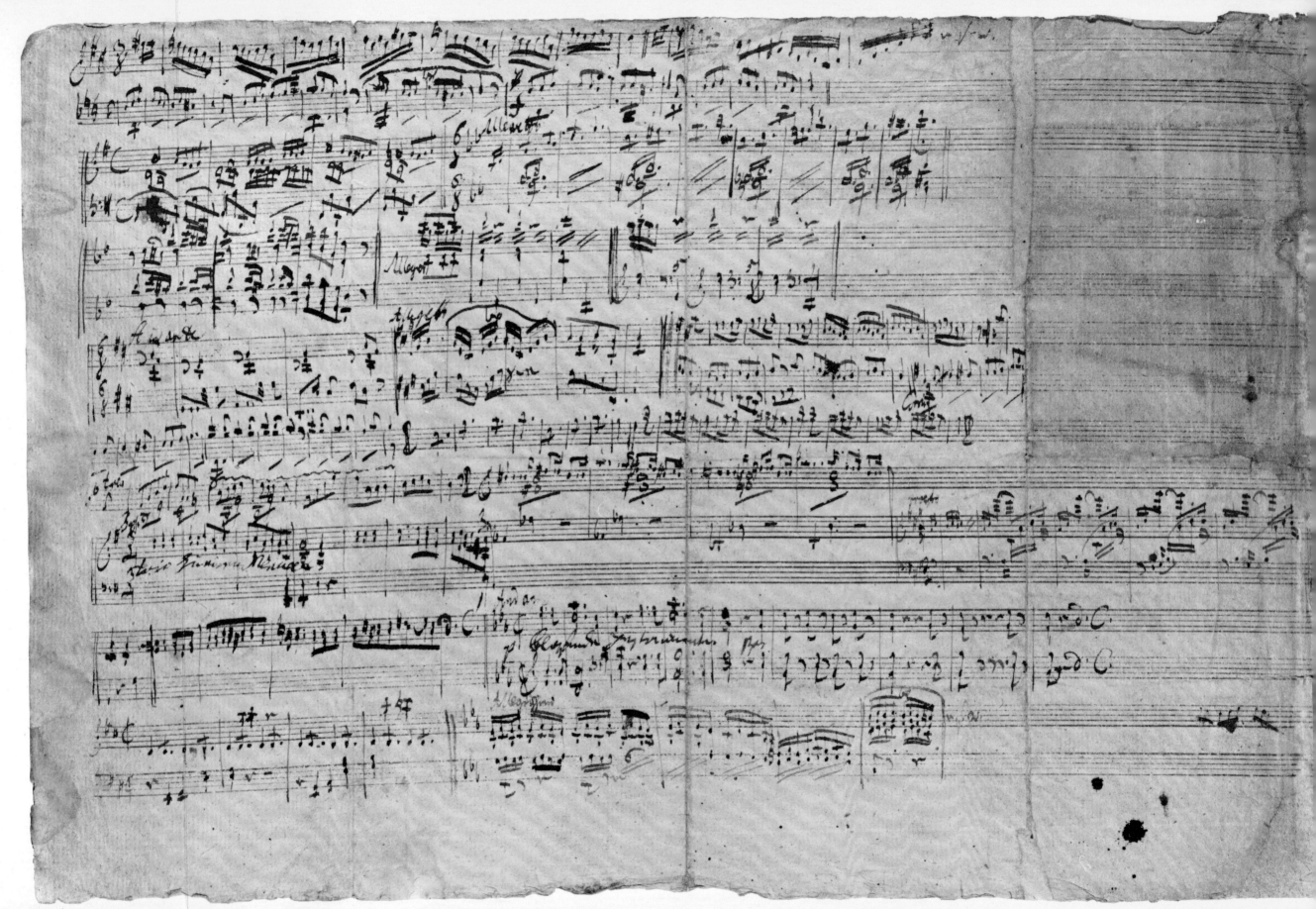

f. 63v

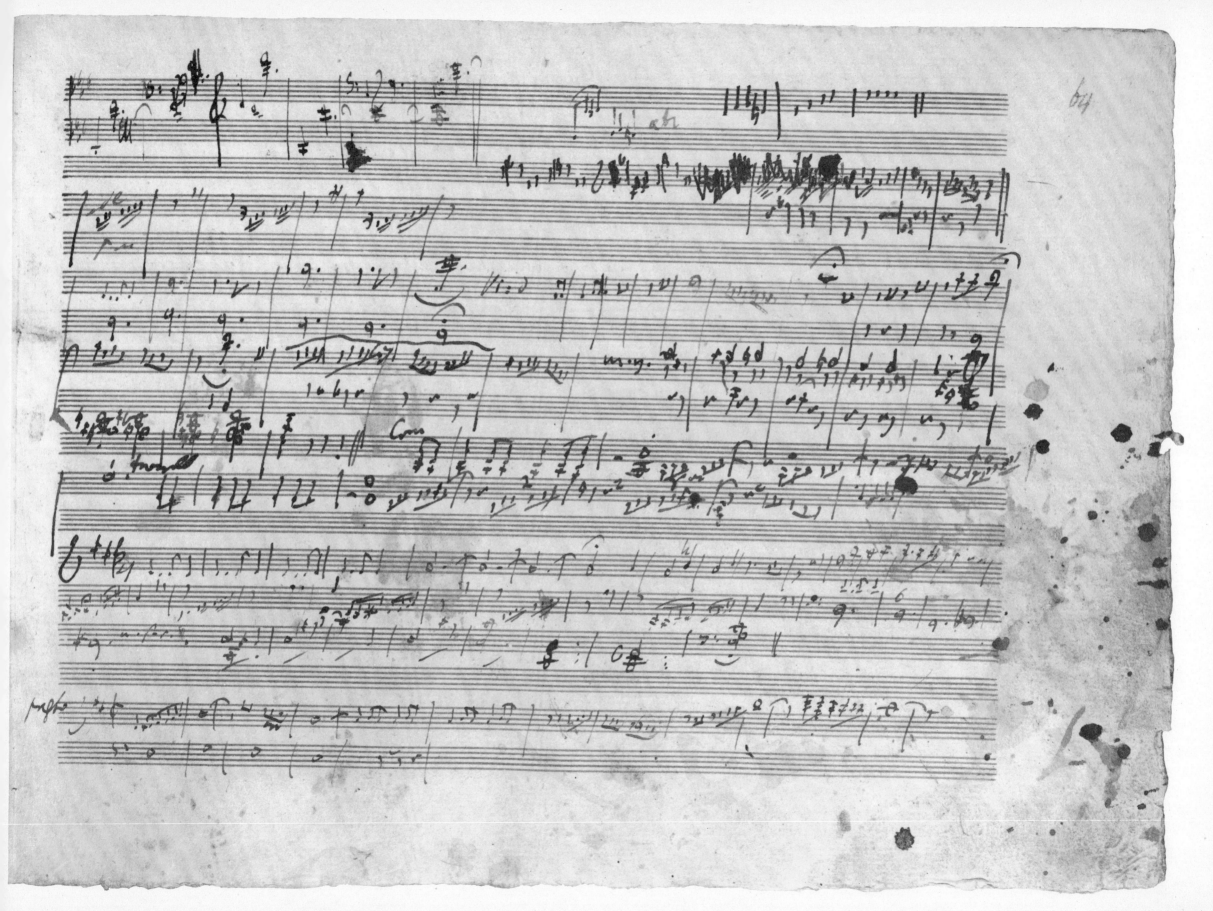

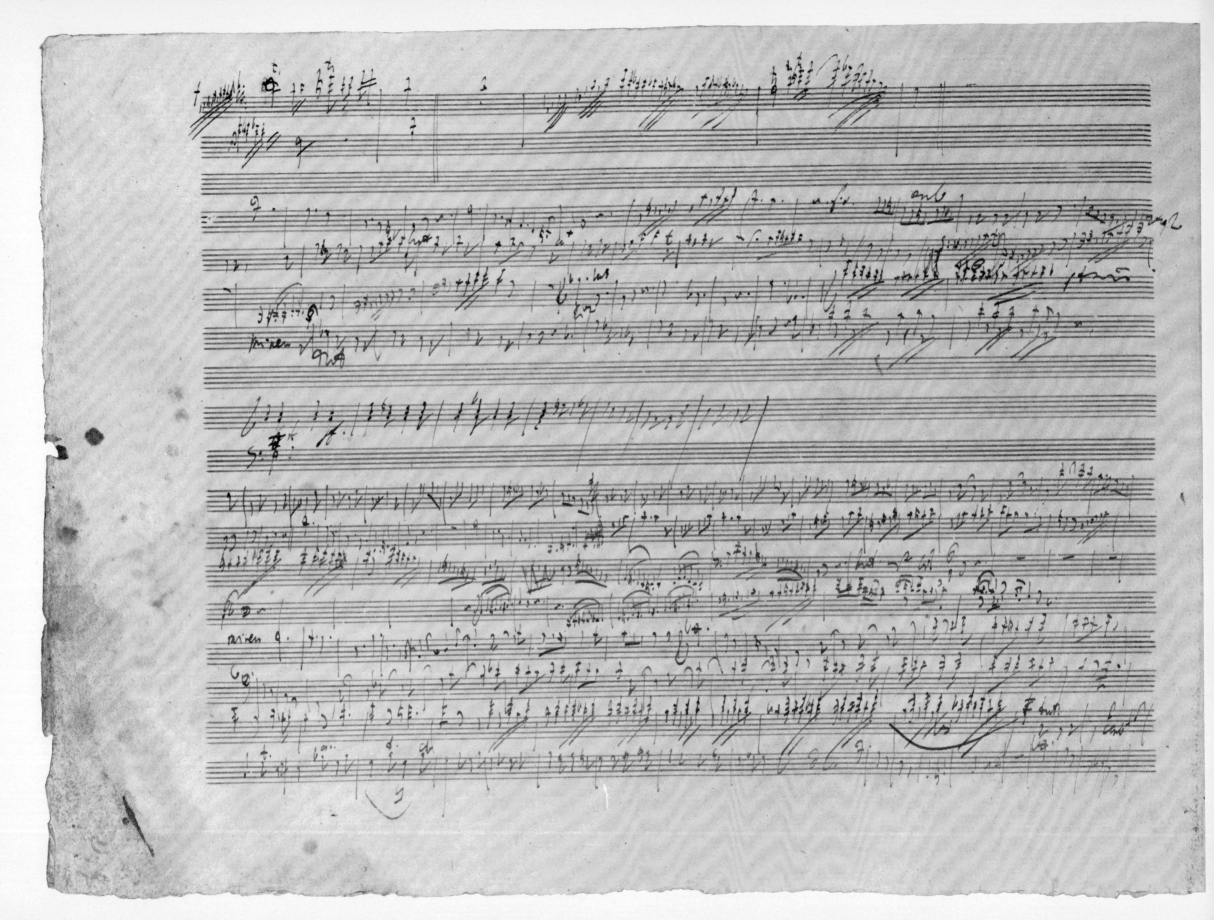

f. 64v

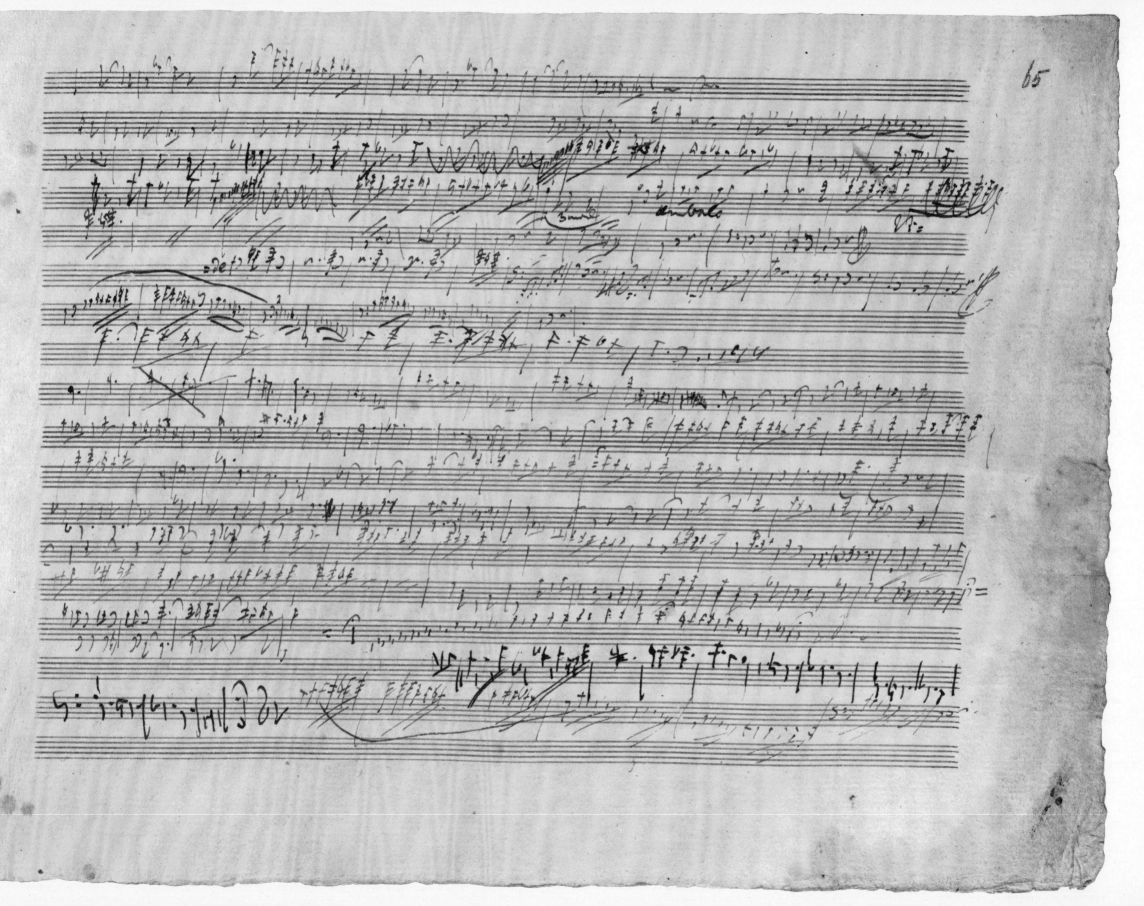

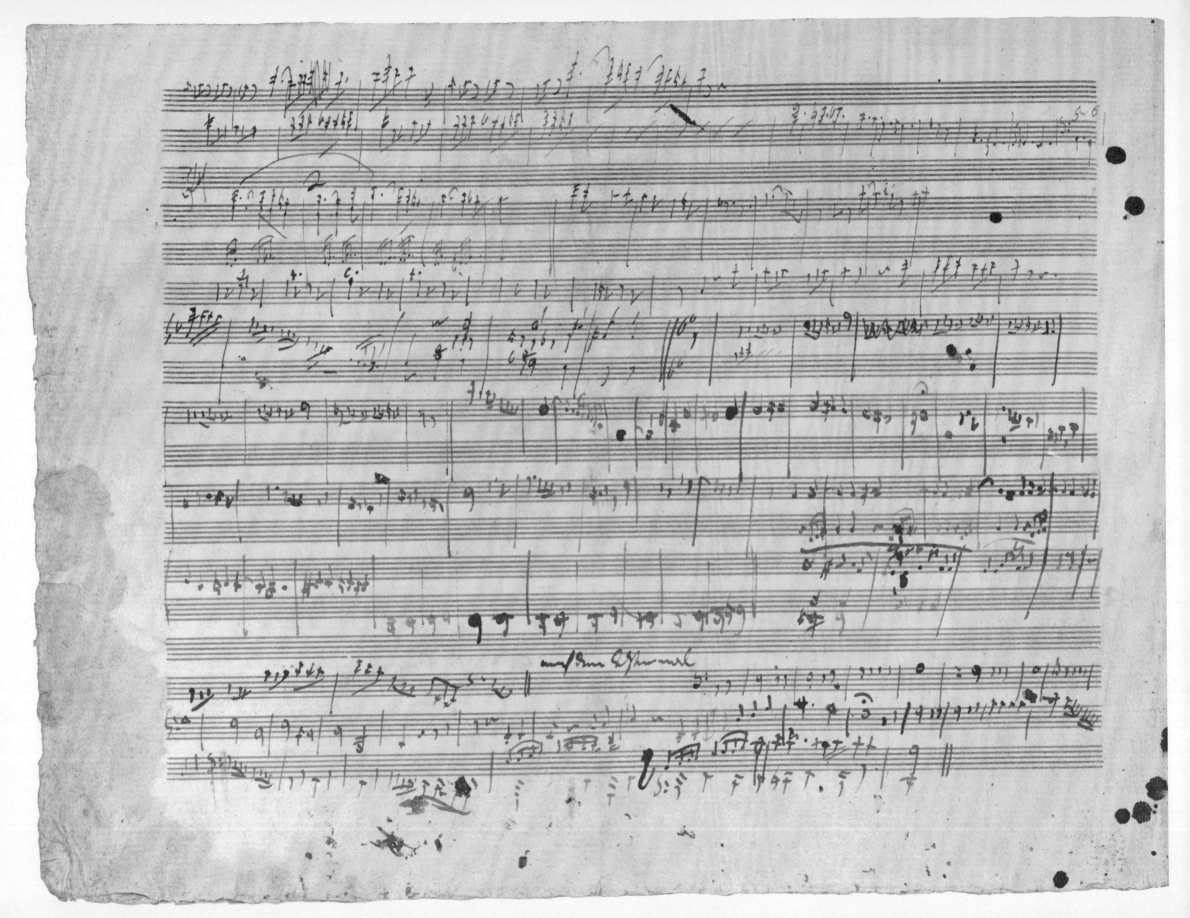

Sonatine.   par C. v. Bthvn.

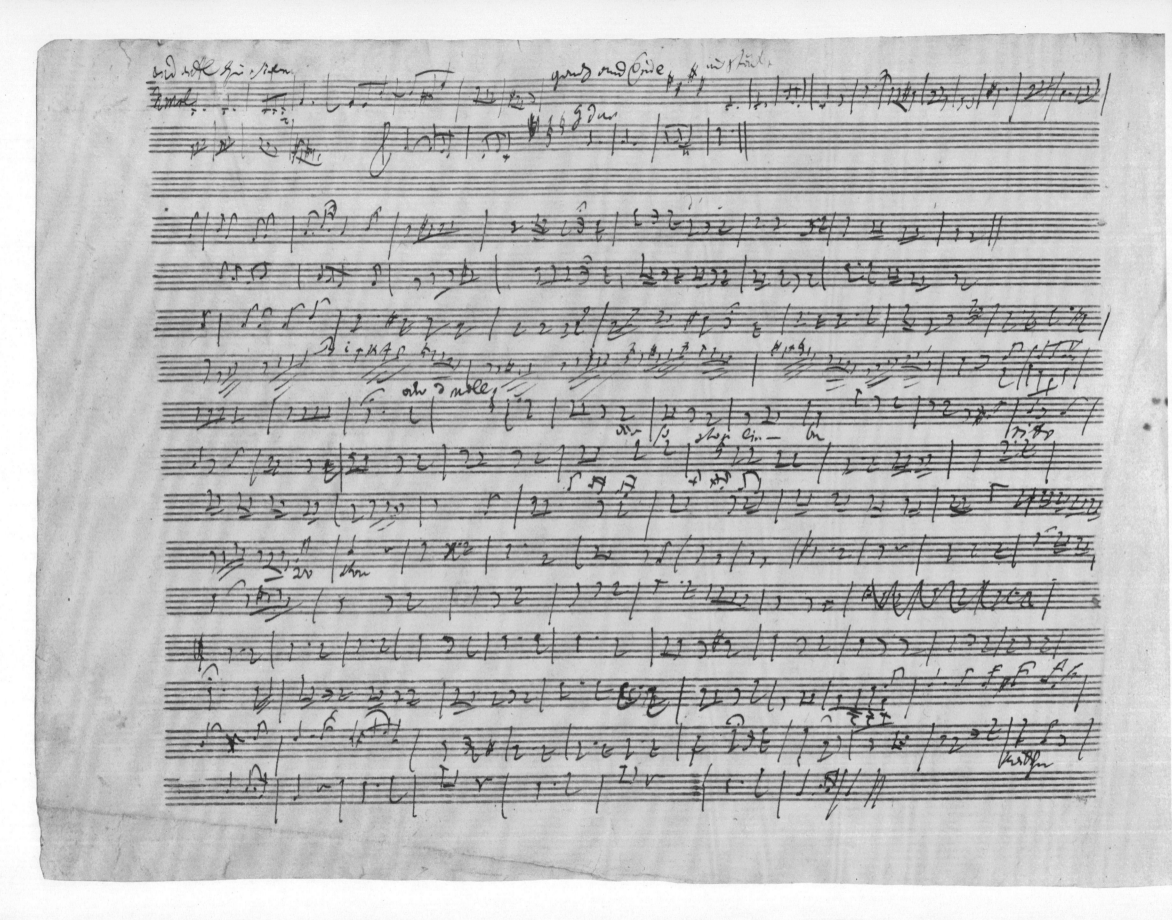

f. 67v

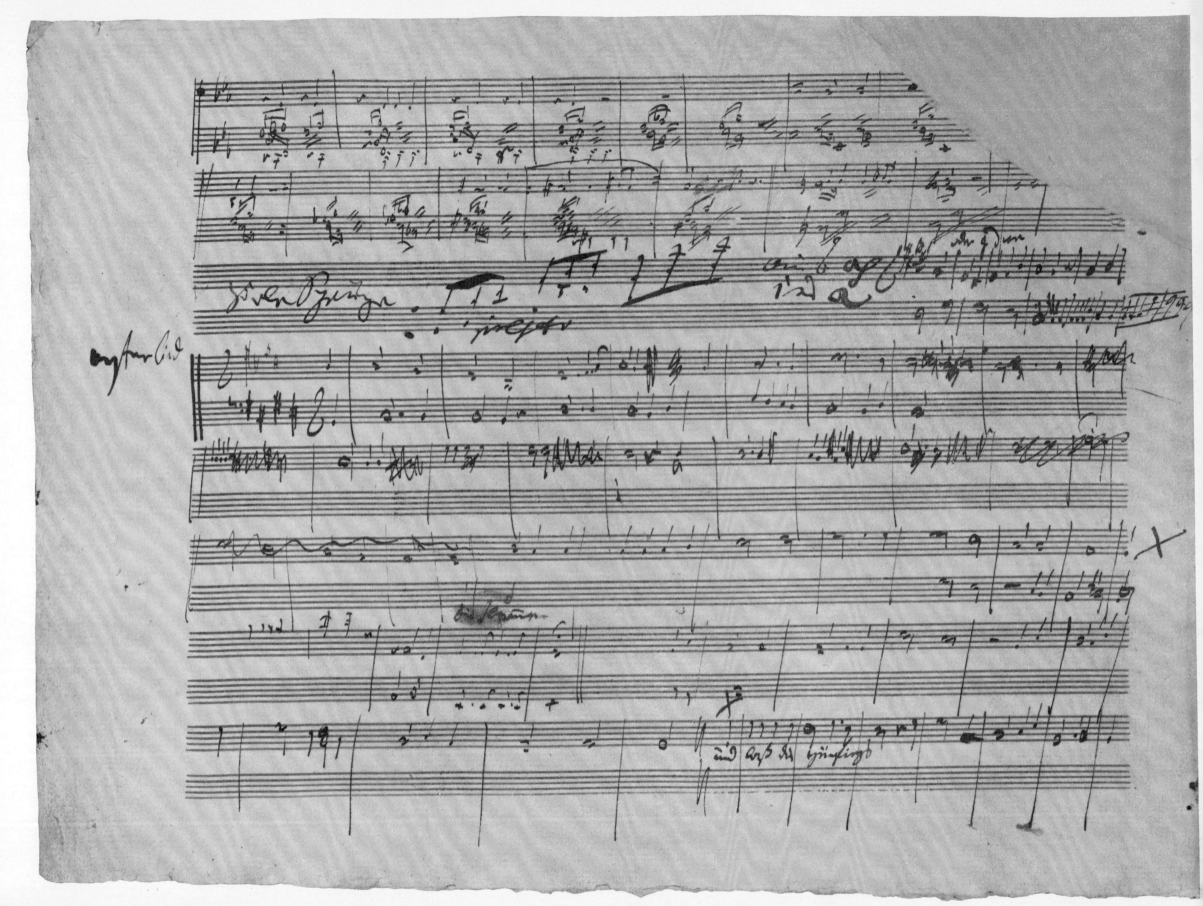

f. 68v

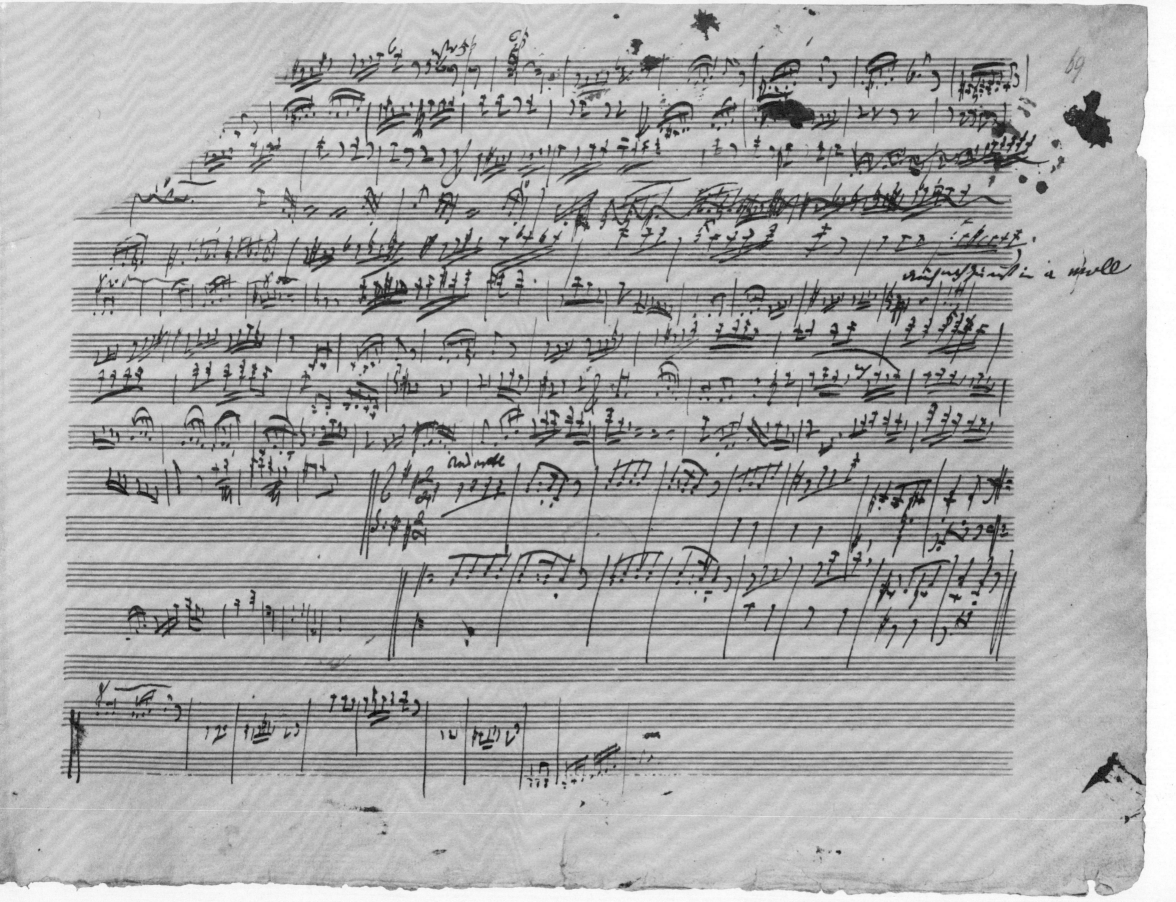

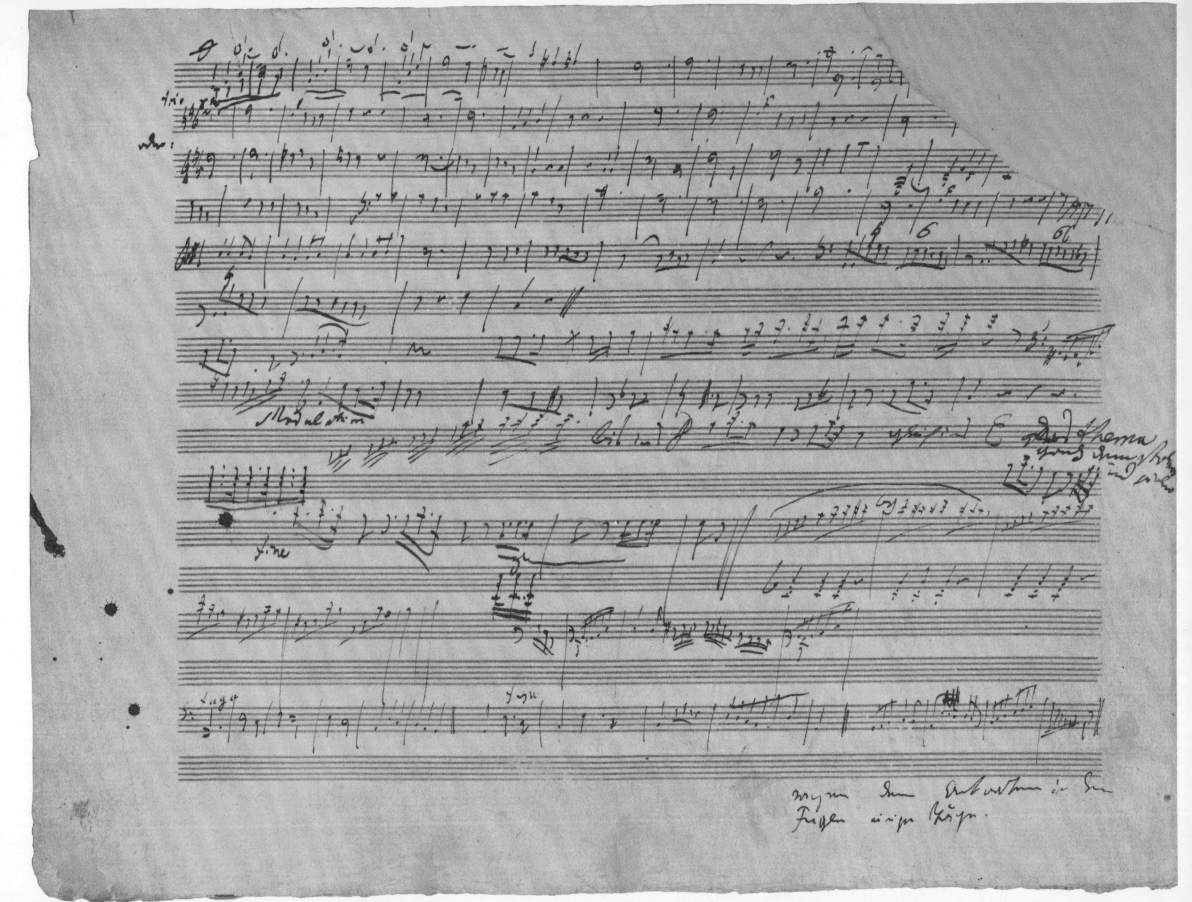

f. 69v

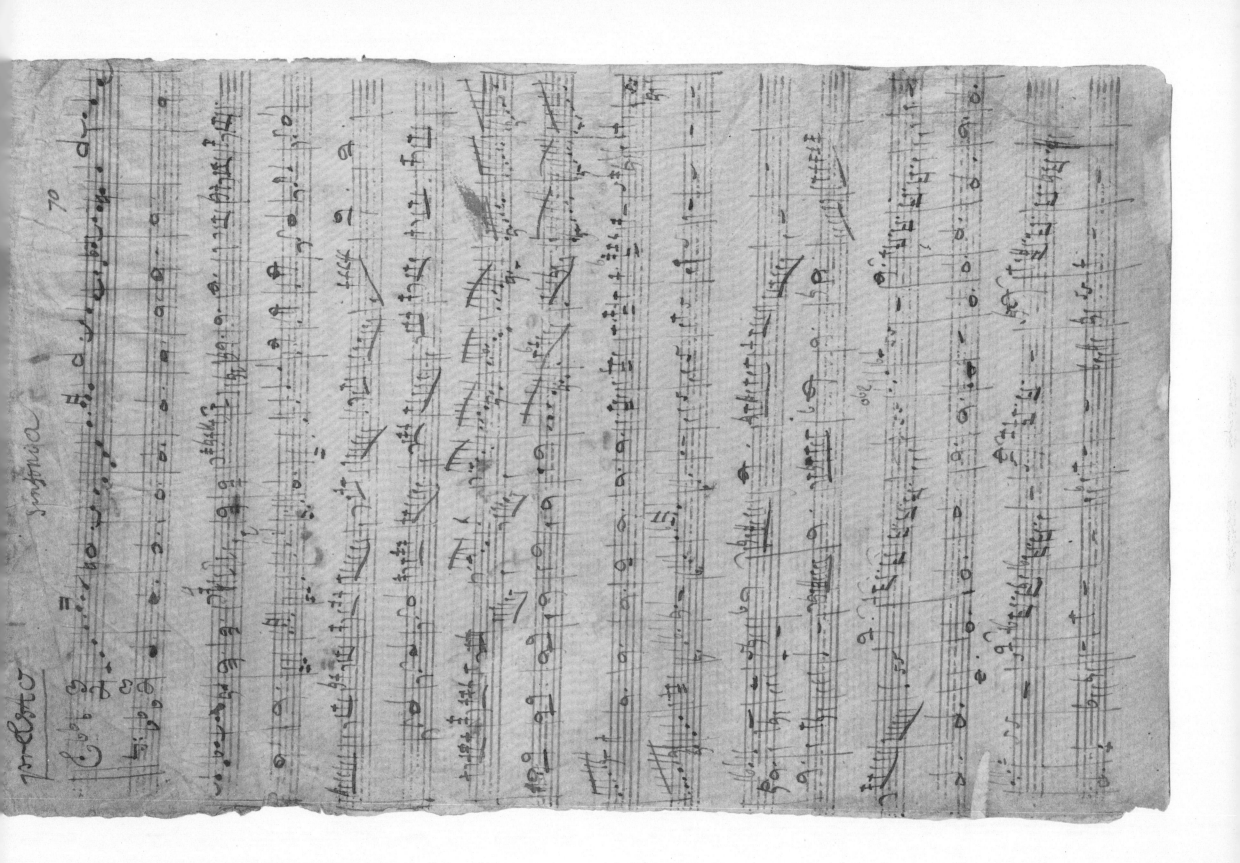

f. 71r

f. 72v

f. 73v

f. 74v

f. 75v

f. 76v

f. 77v

f. 78v

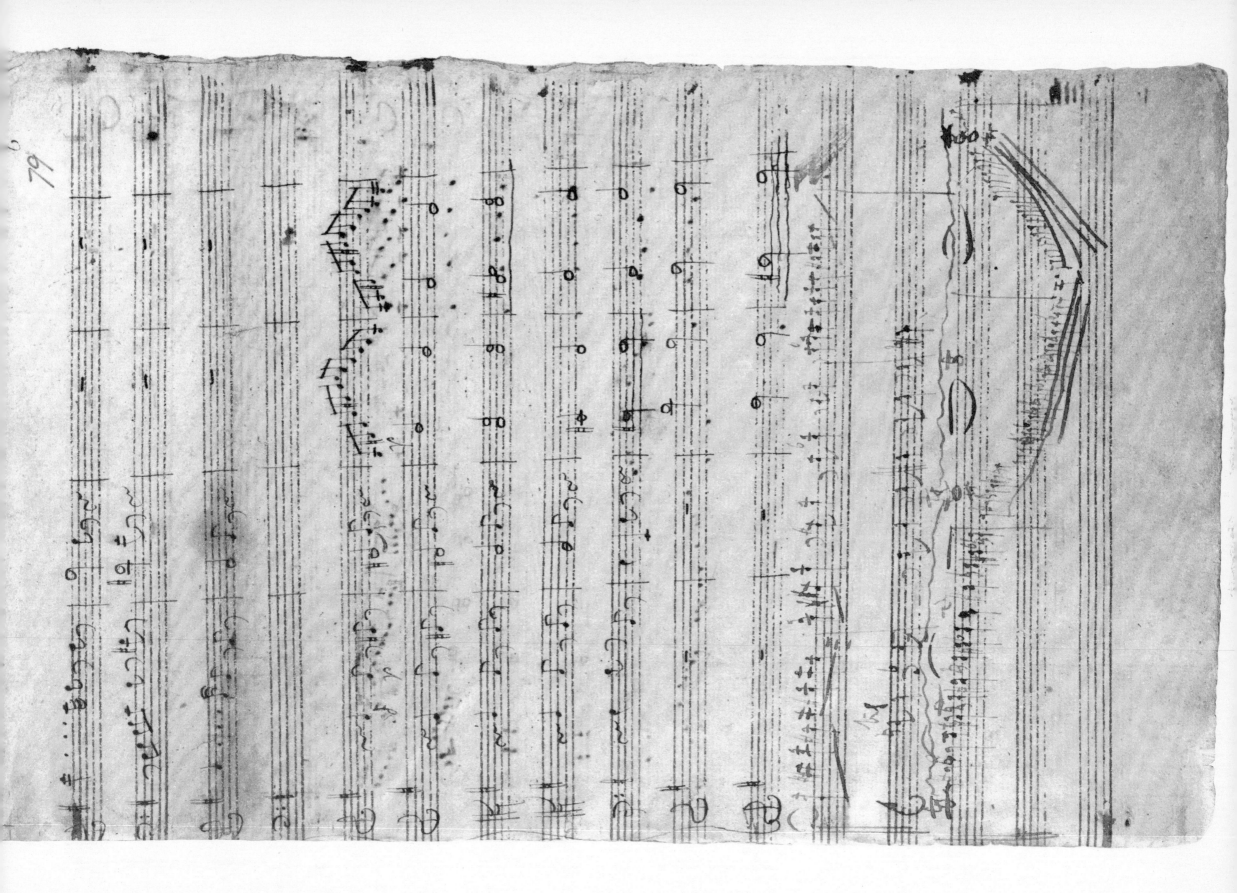

Segue maggiore

f. 81v

f. 83v

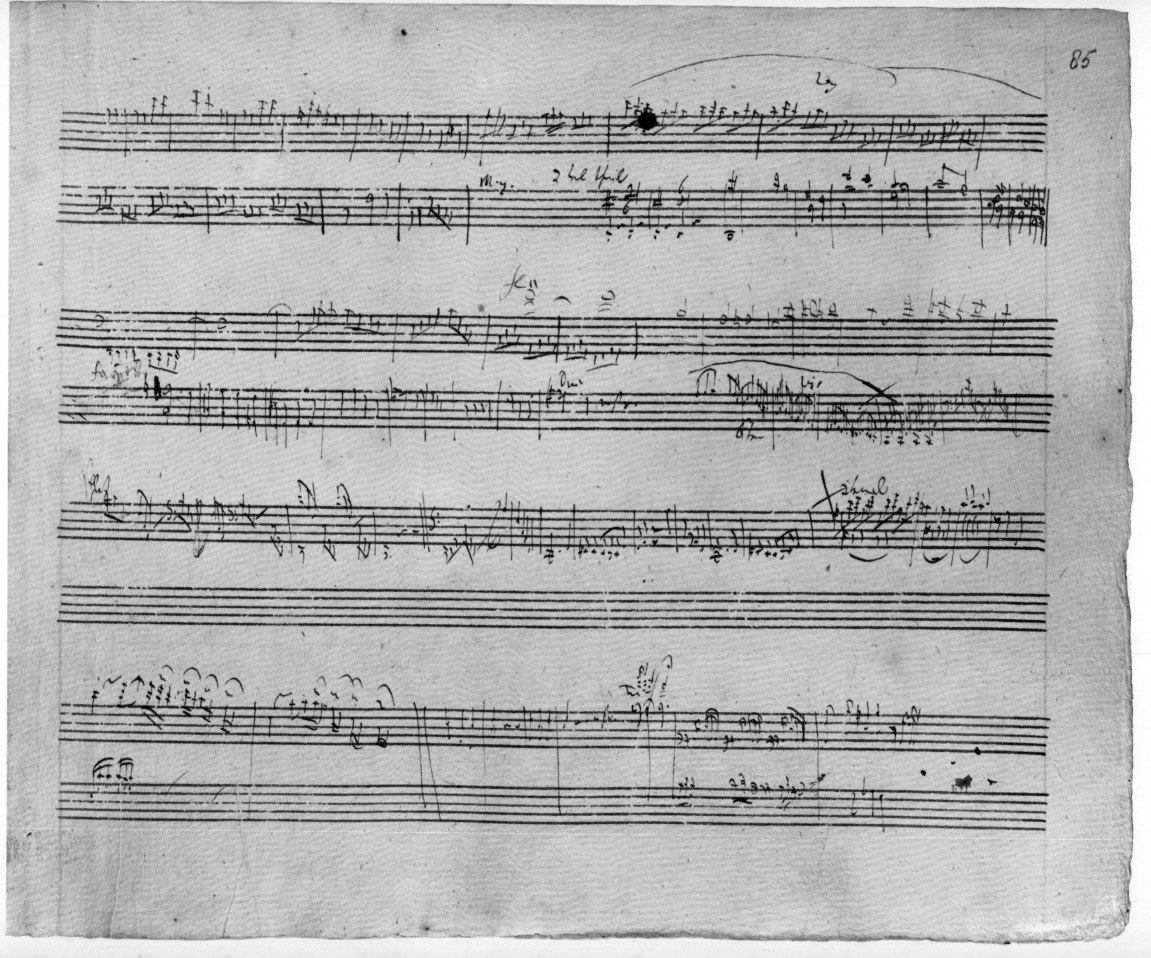

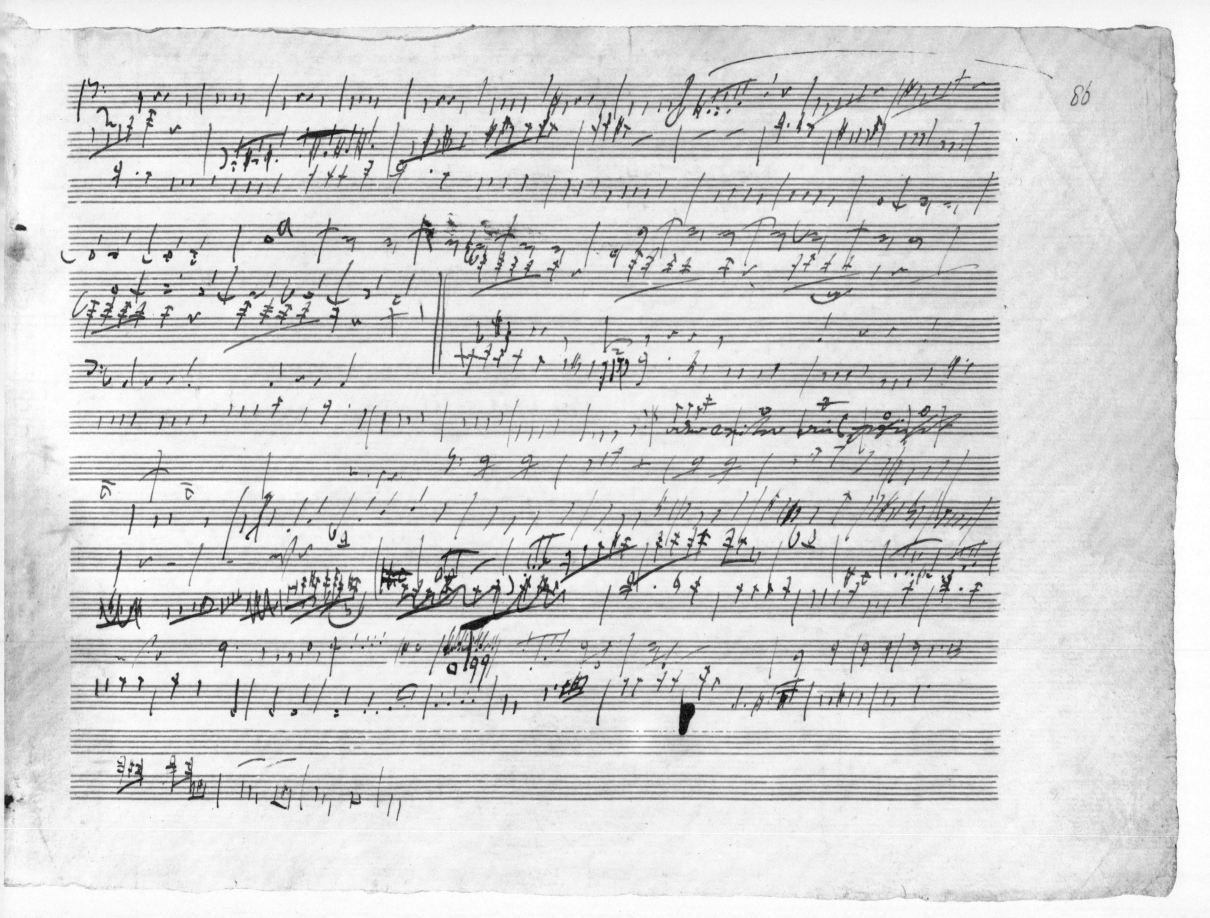

f. 86v

Adagio

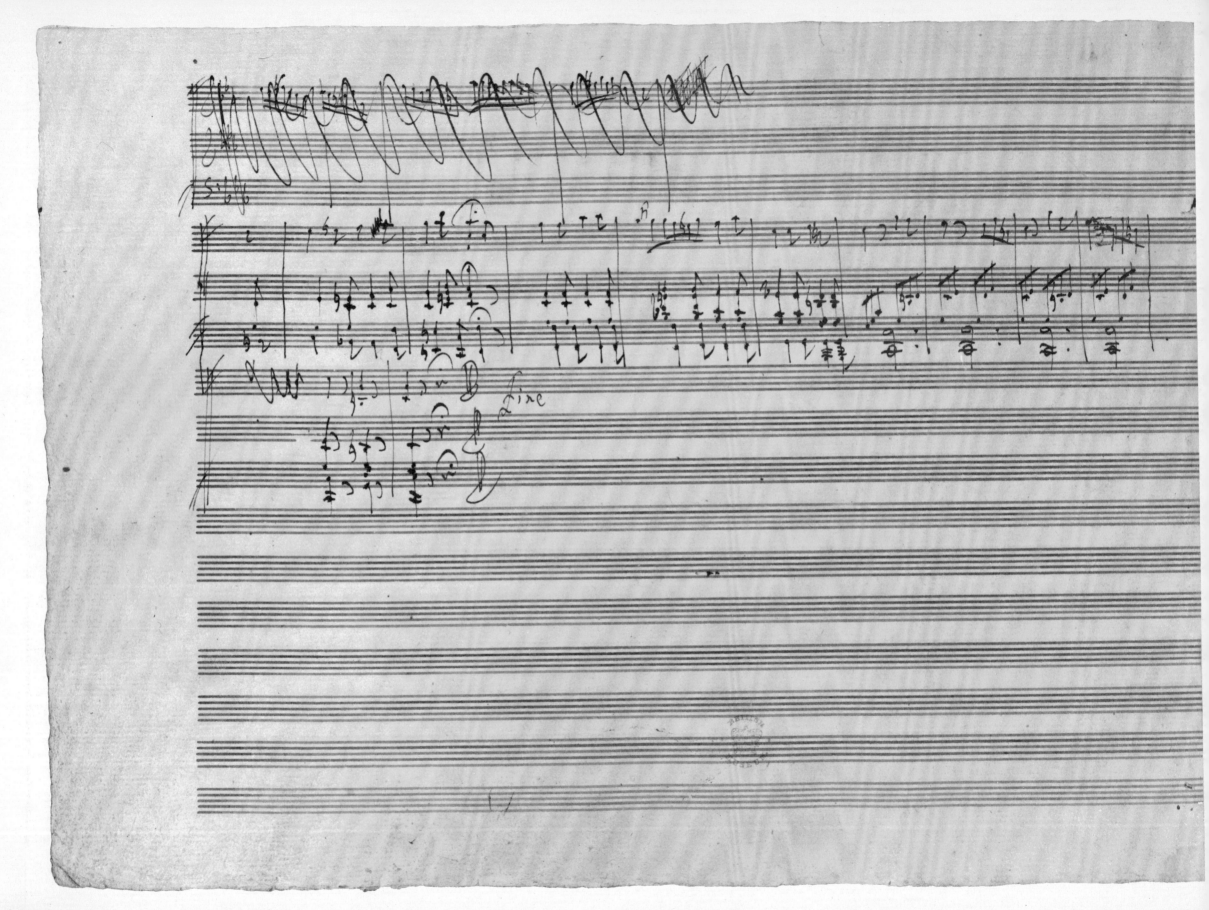

f. 88v

f. 89v

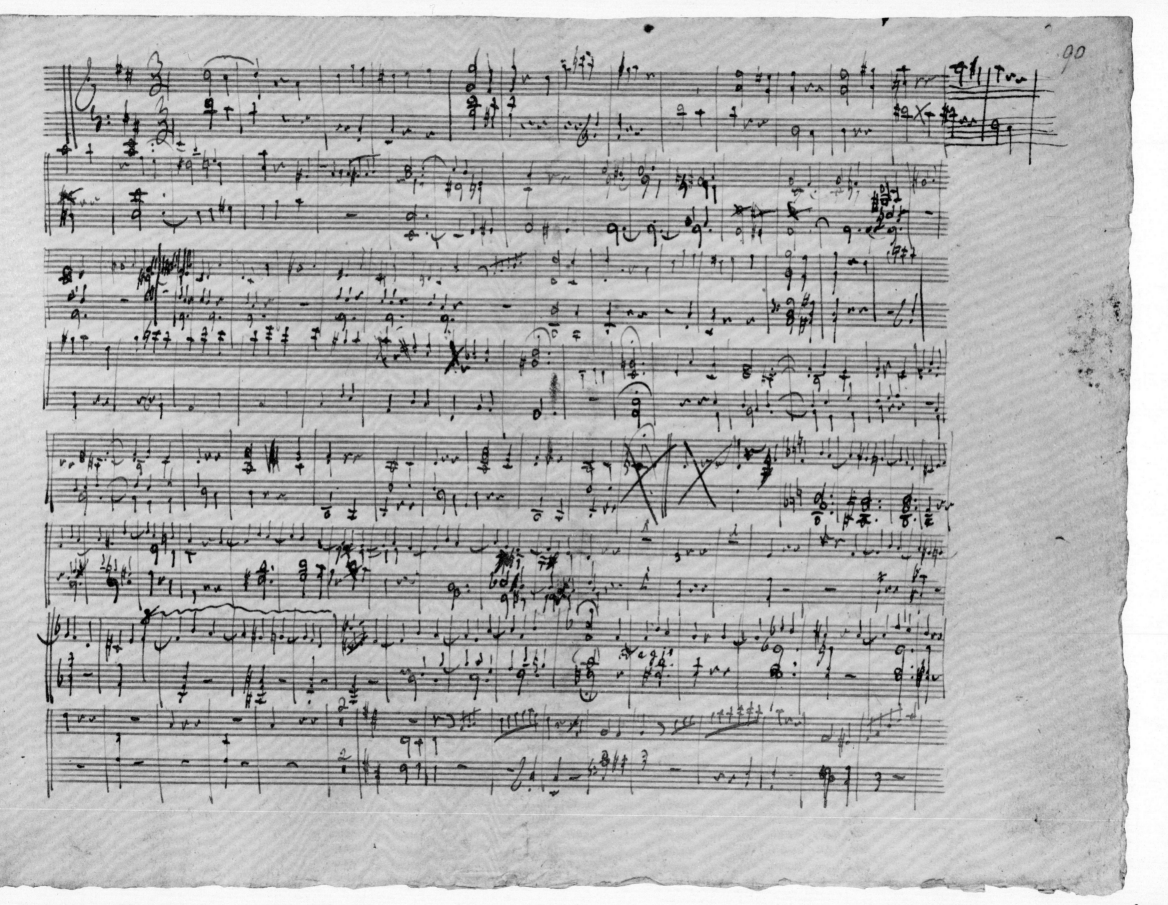

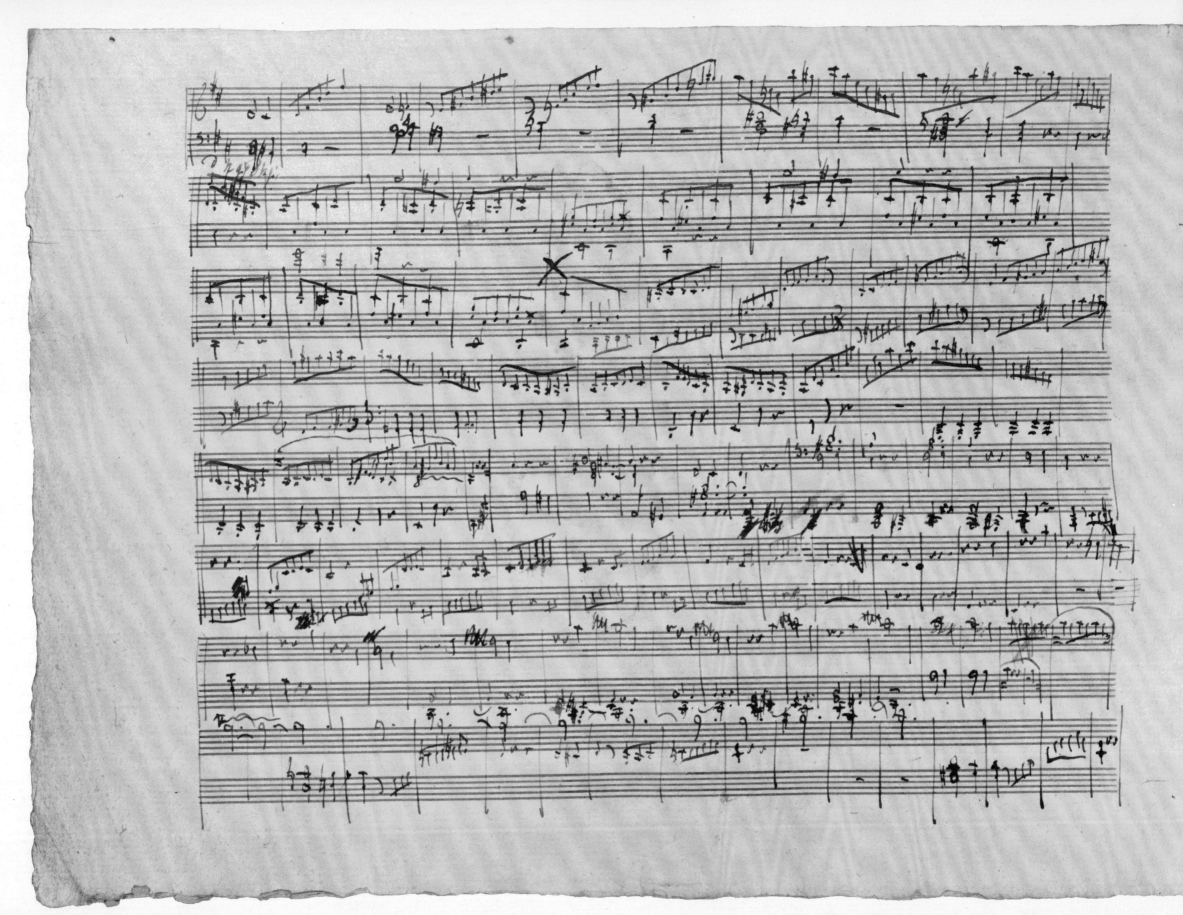

f. 90v

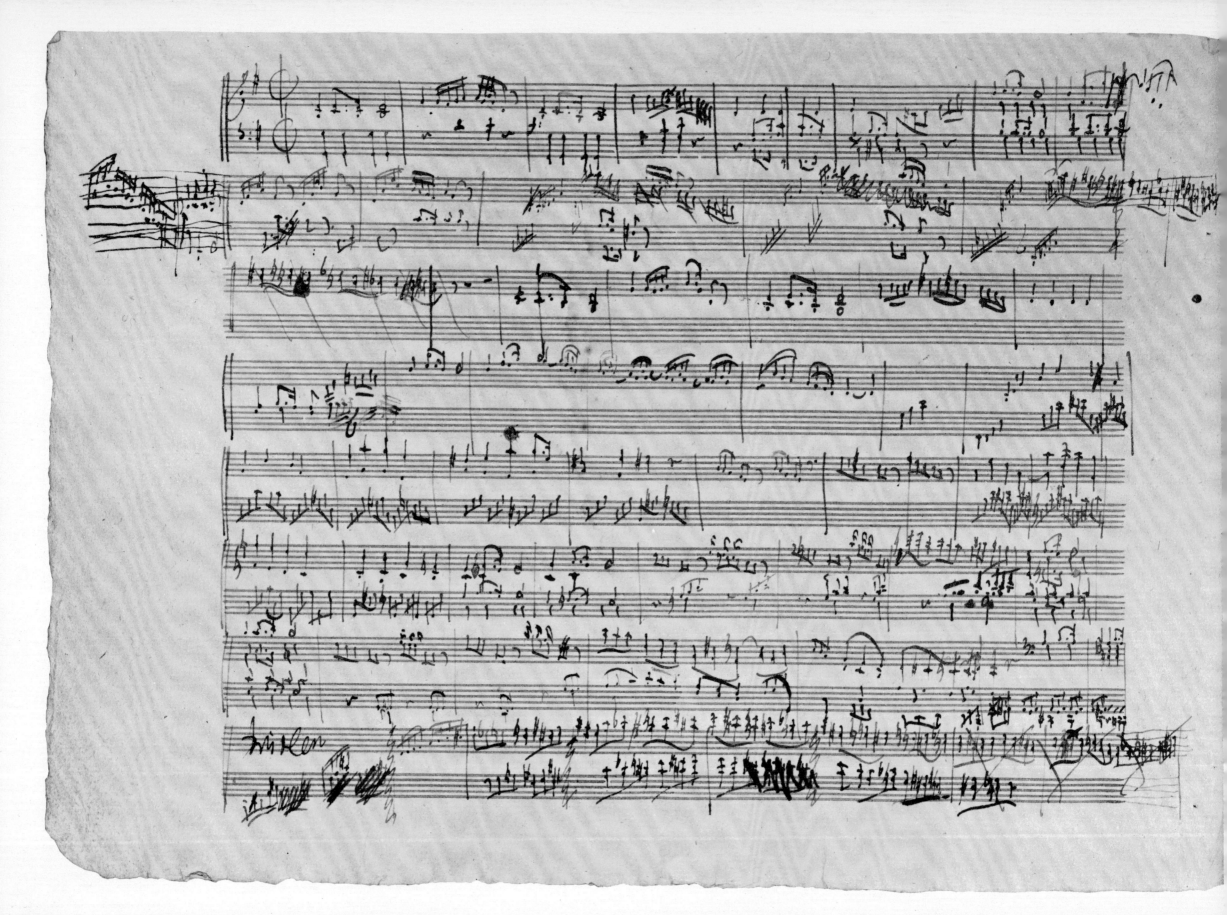

f. 91v

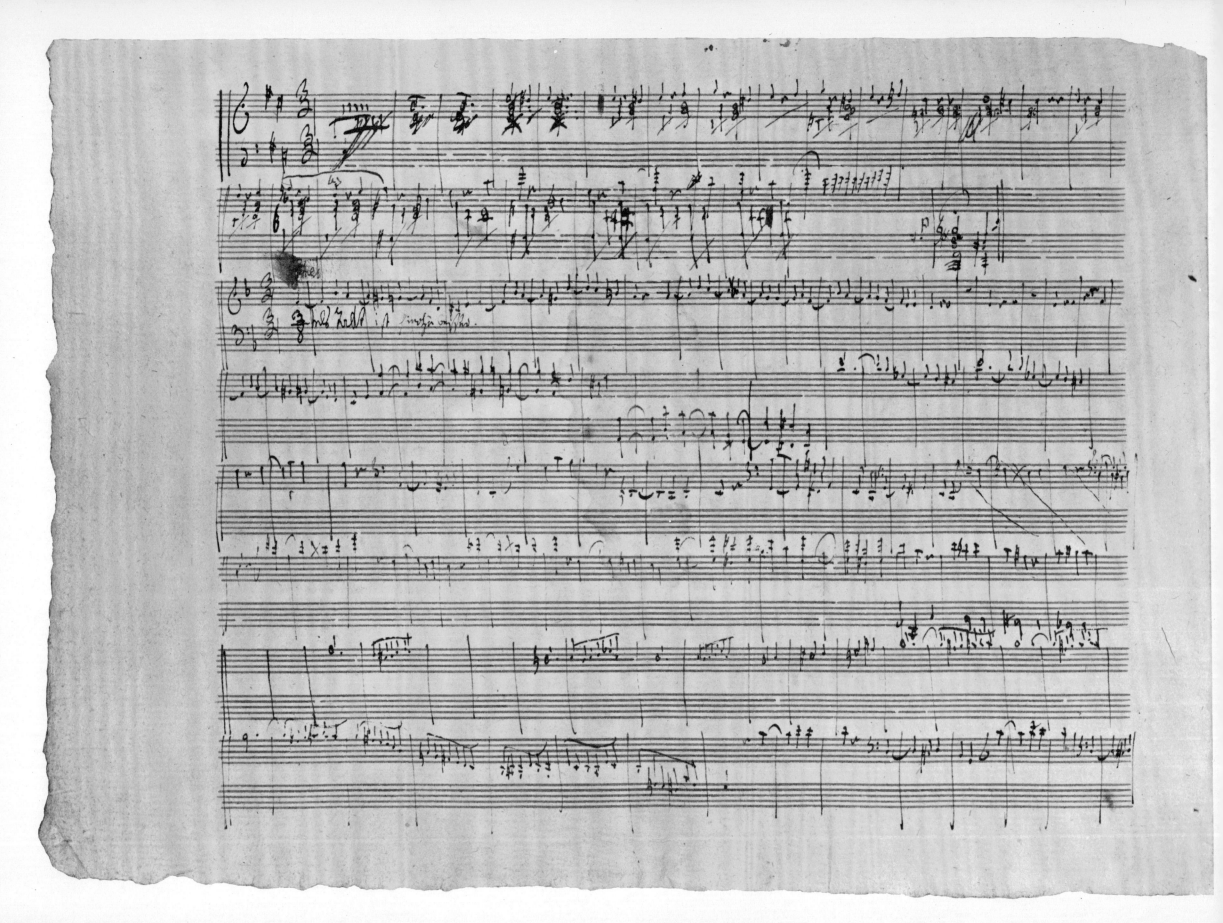

f. 92v

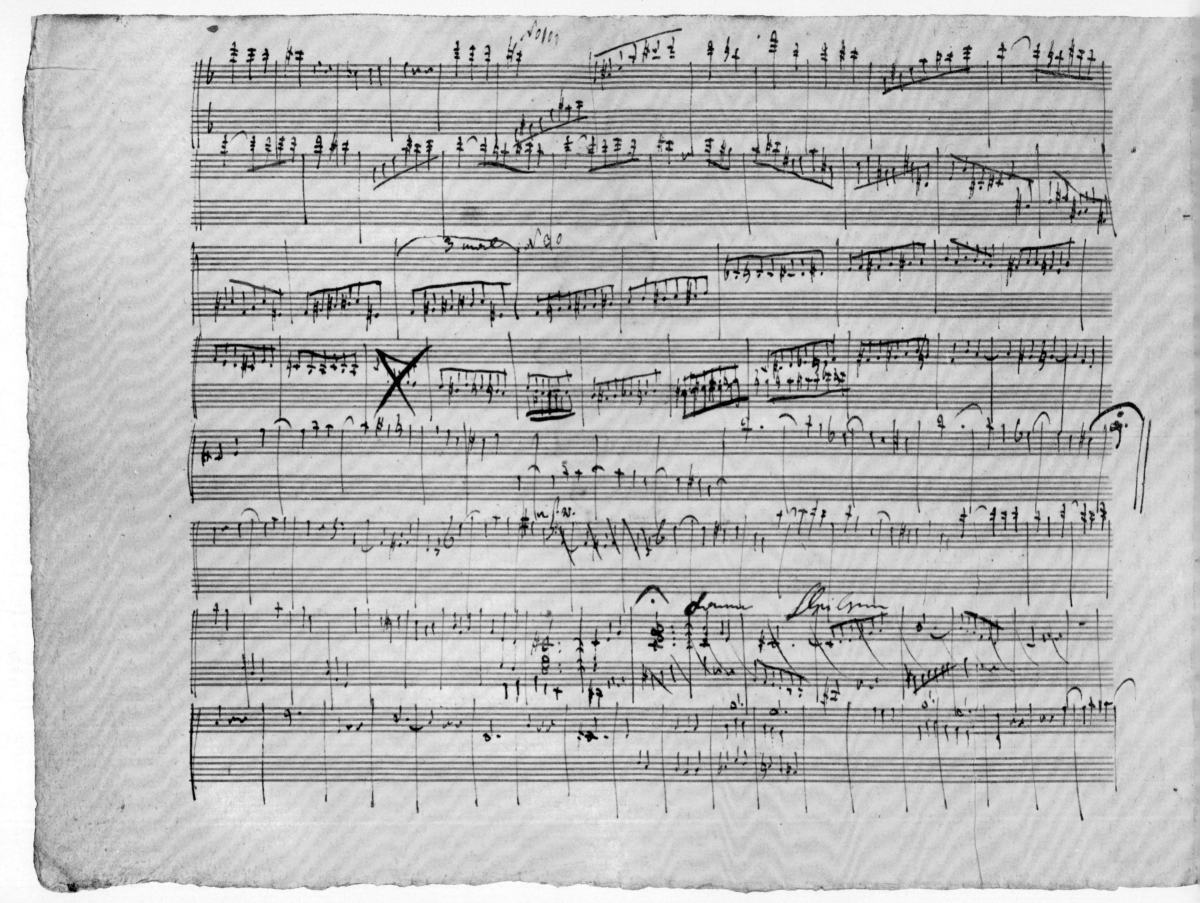

f. 93v

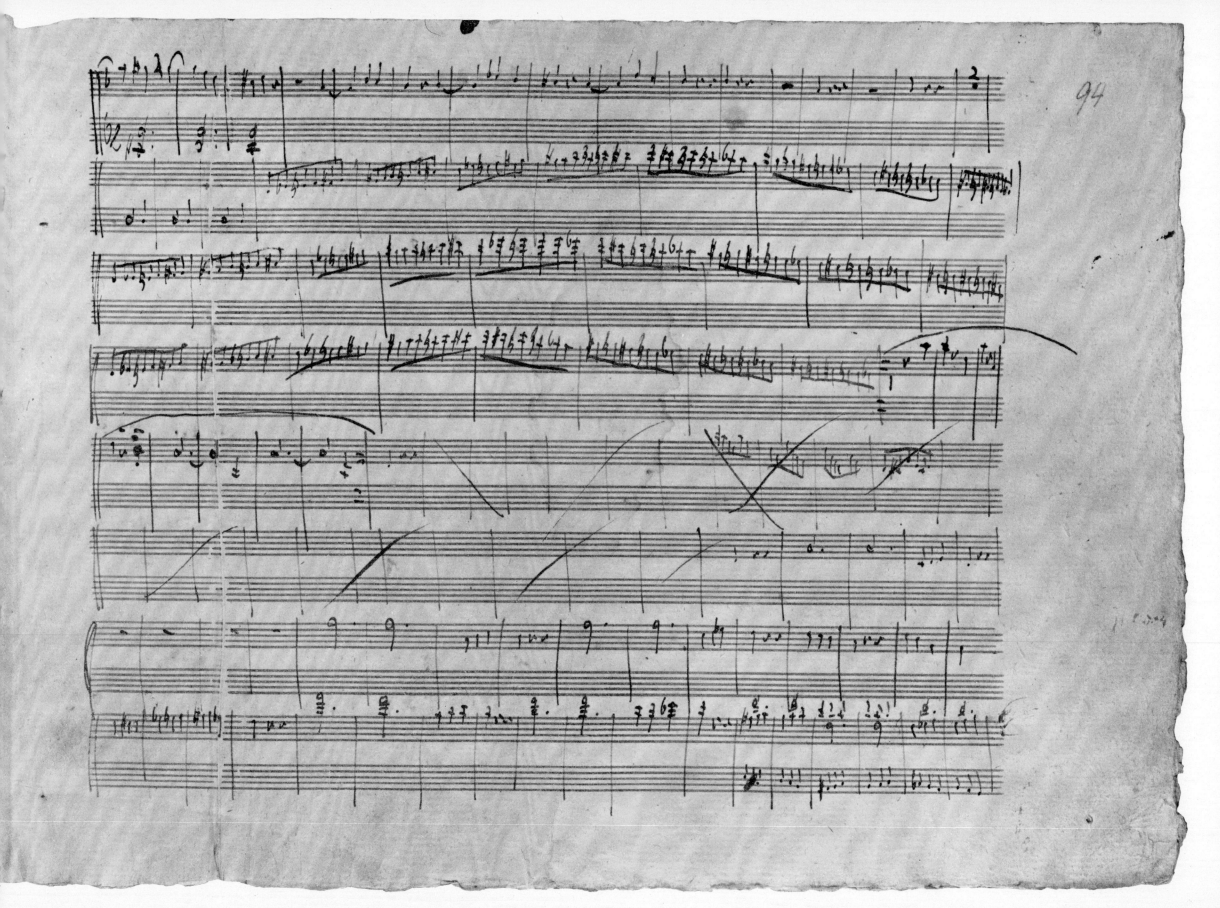

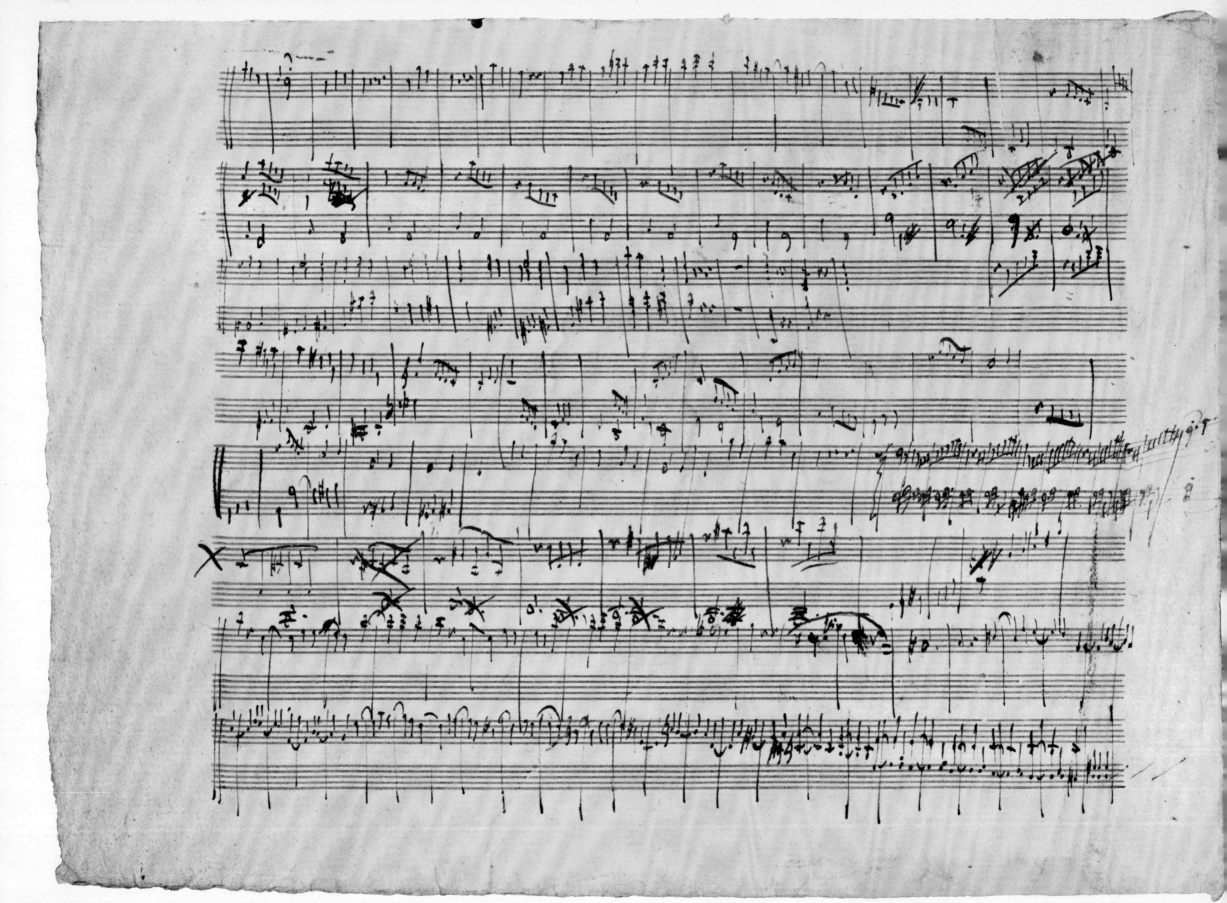

f. 95v

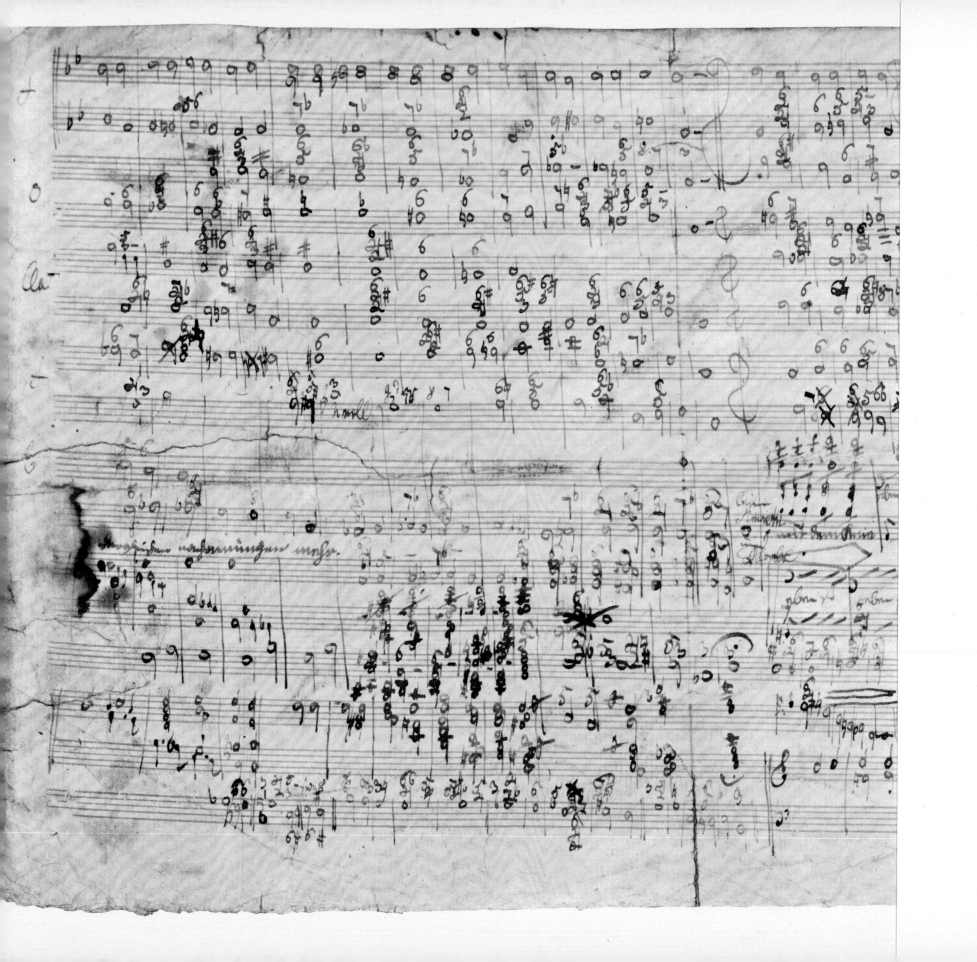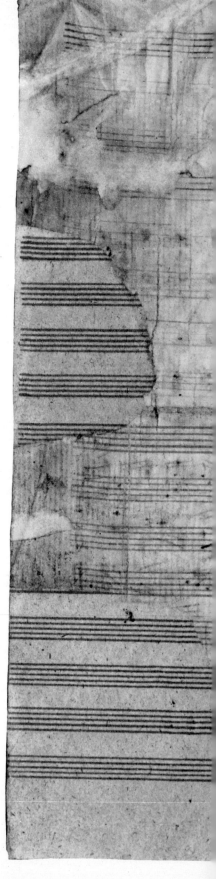

f. 96v

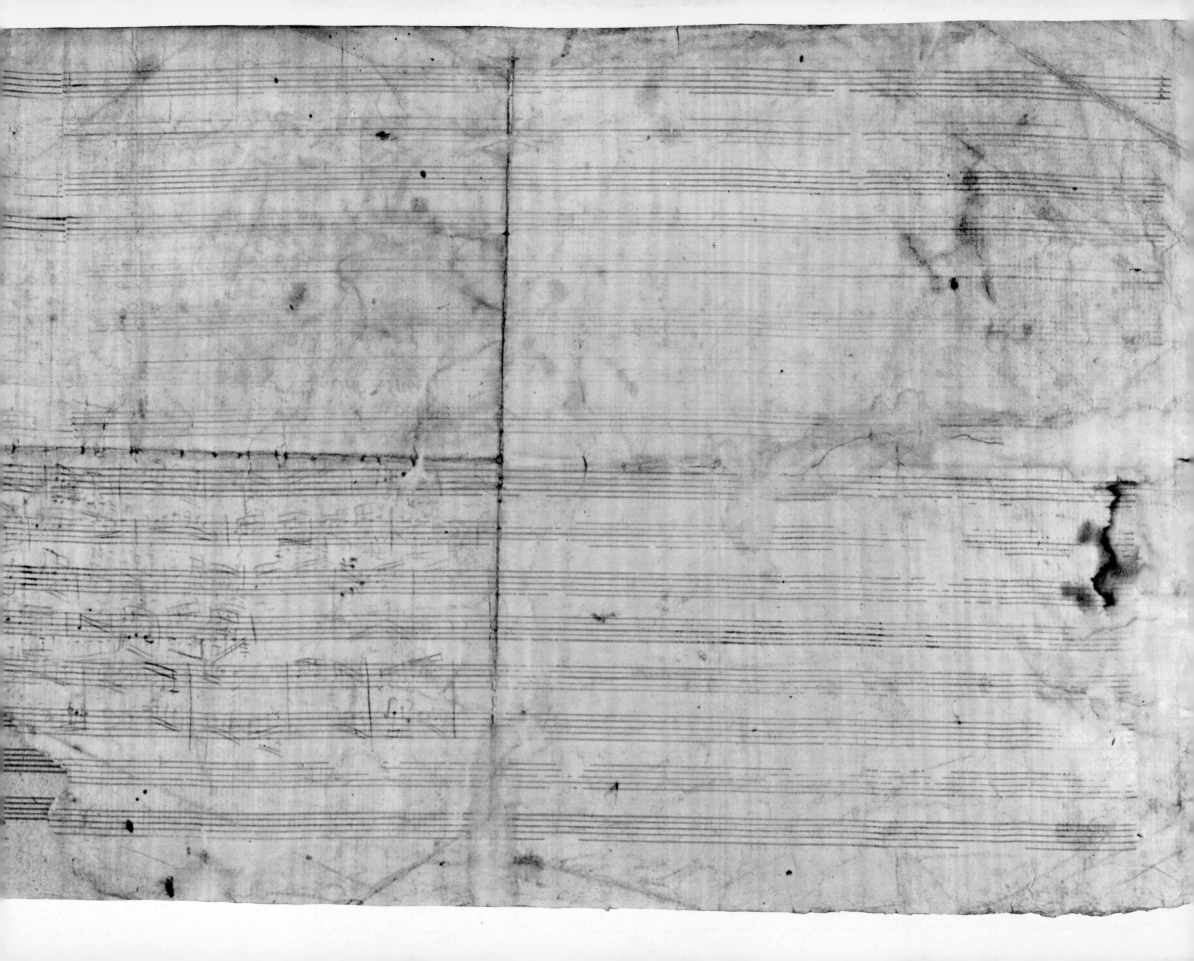

f. 98v

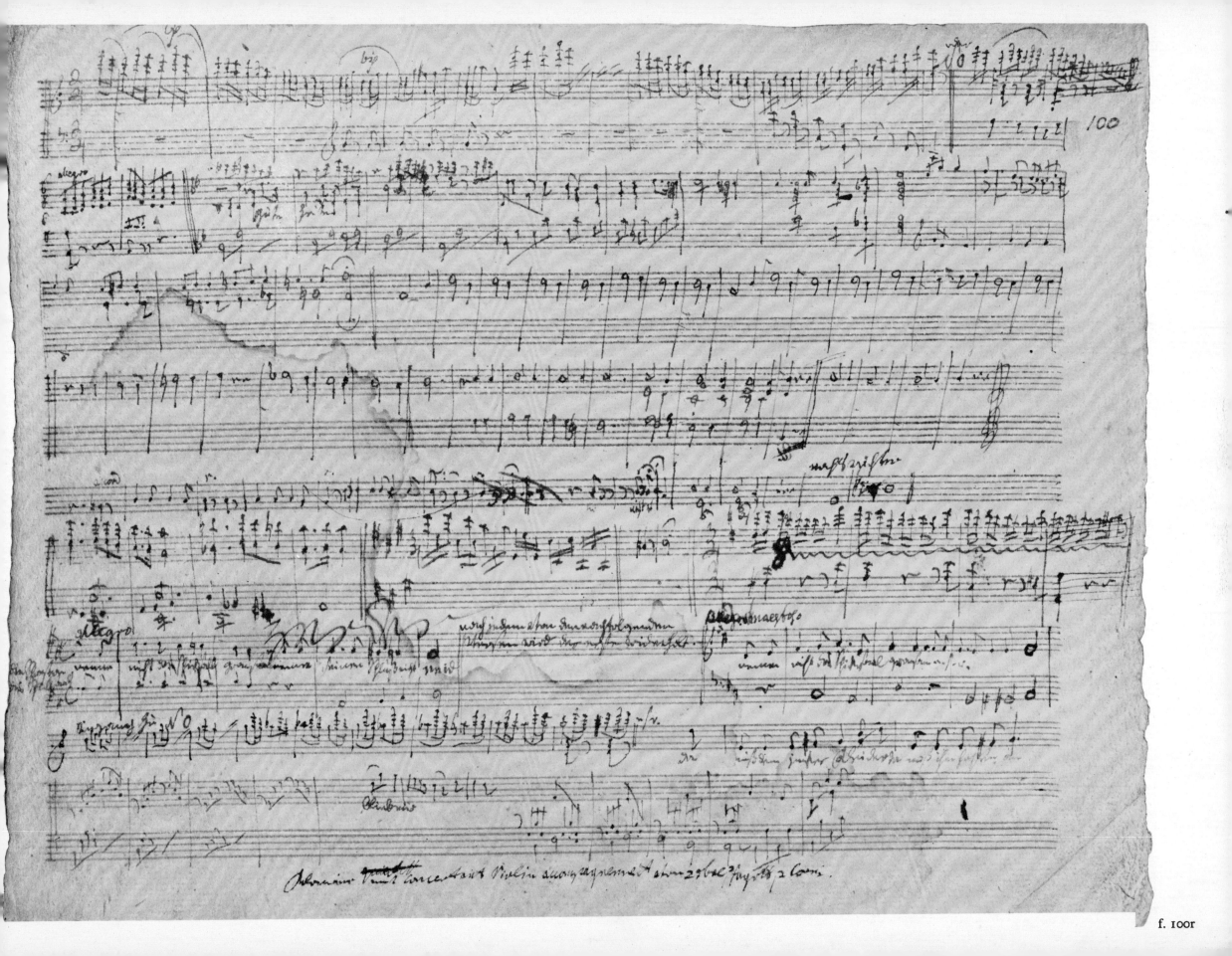

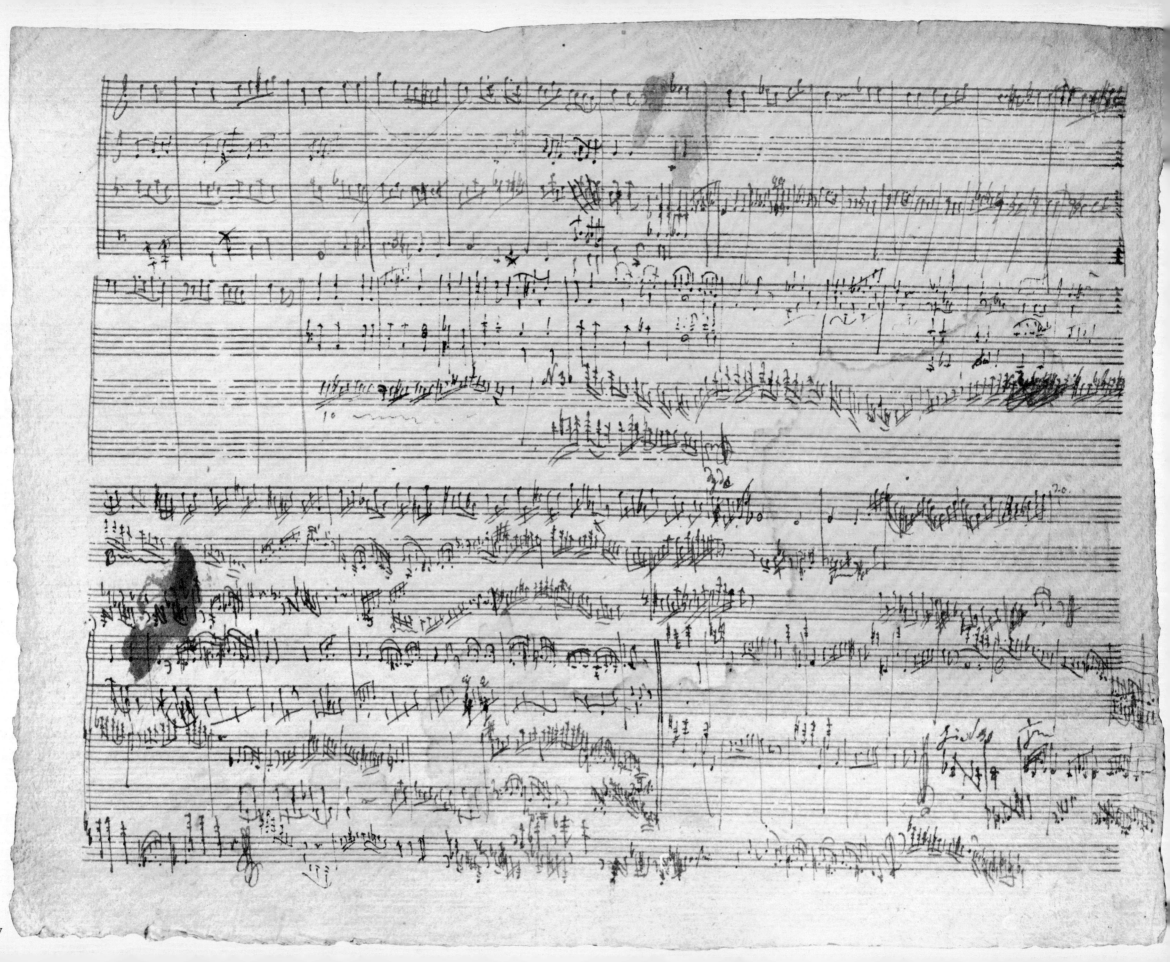

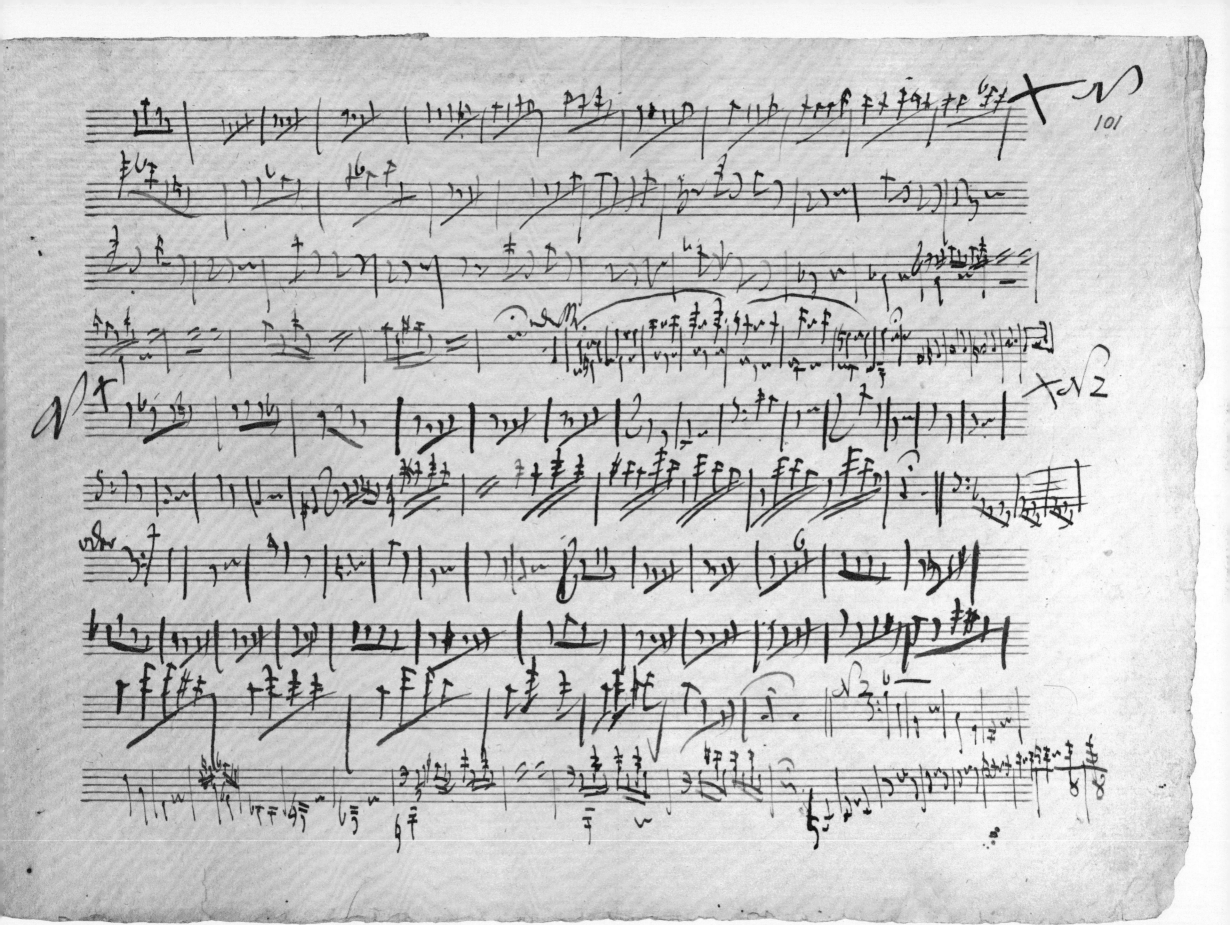

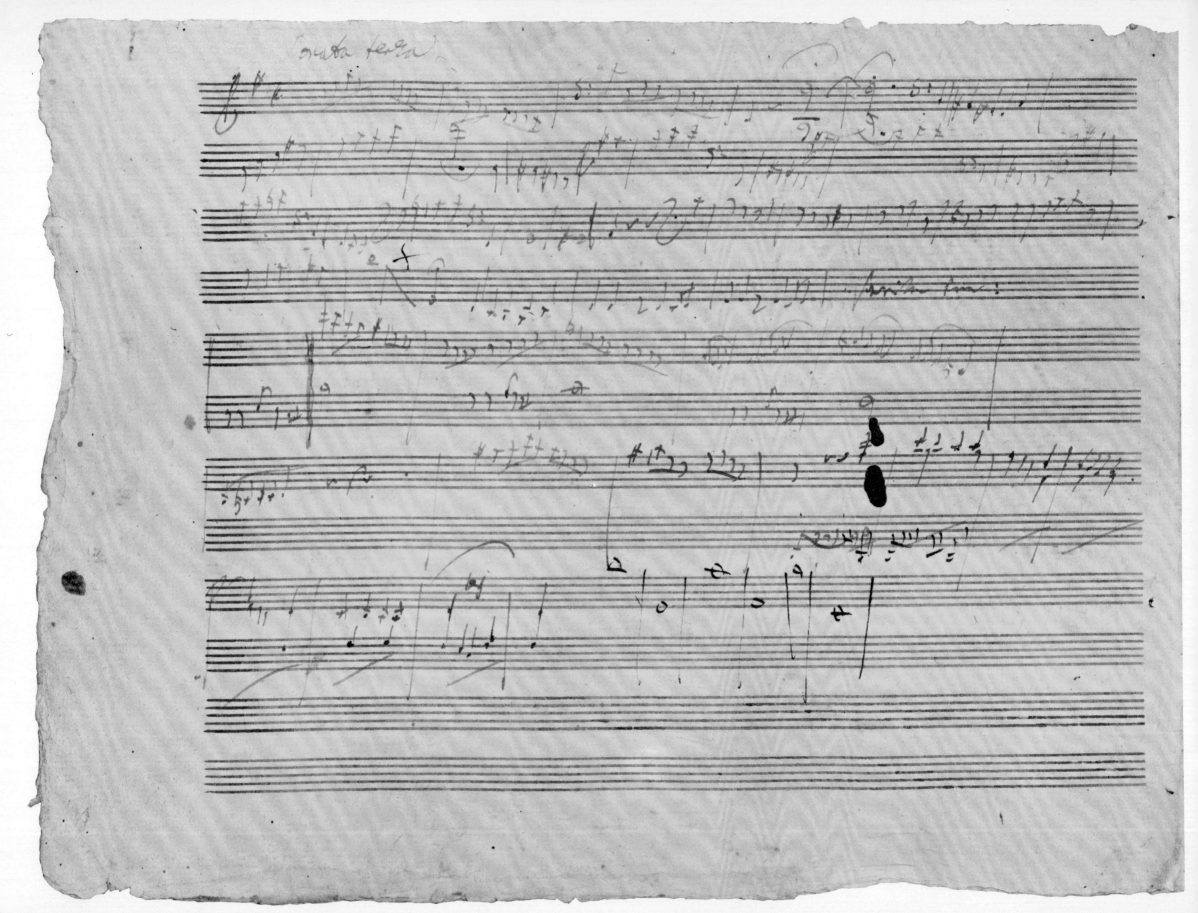

f. 103v

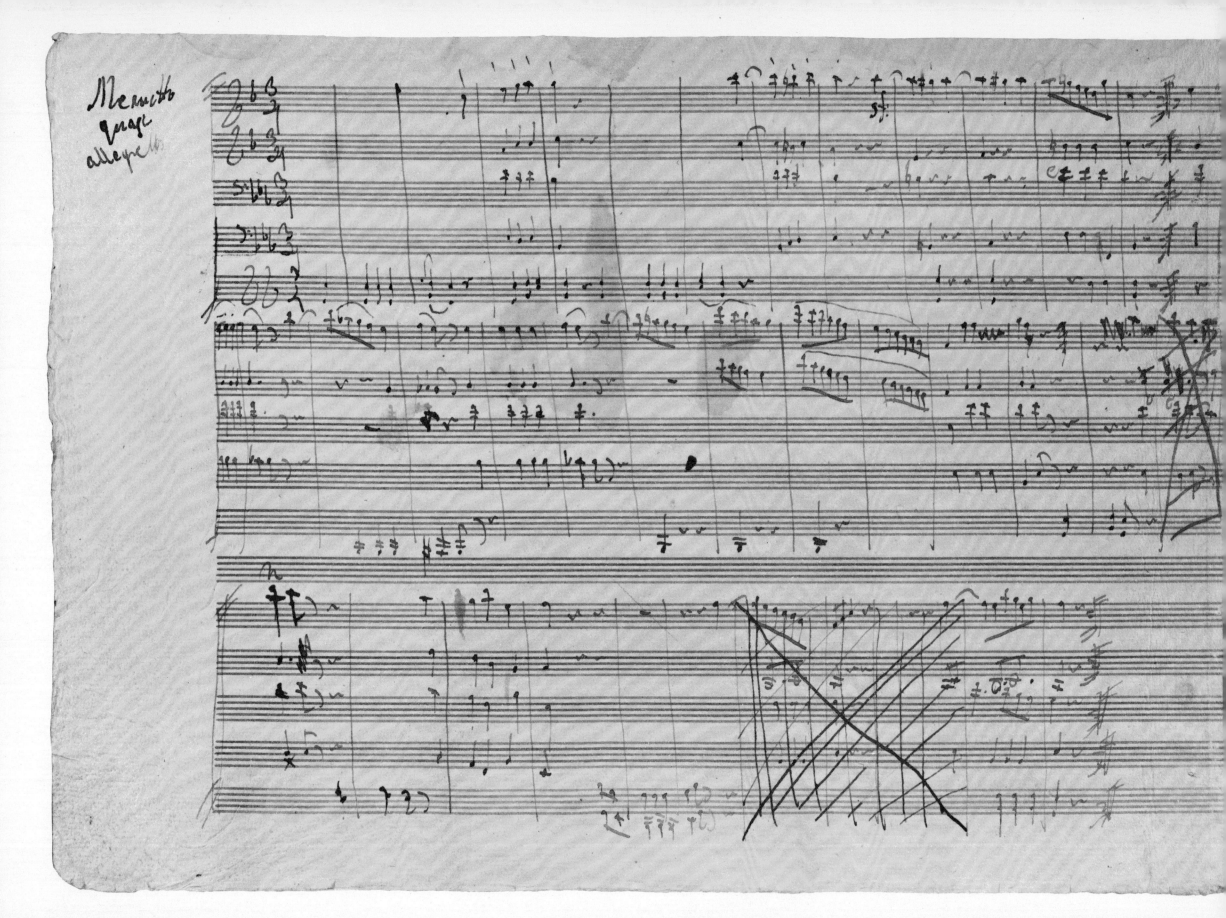

f. 105v

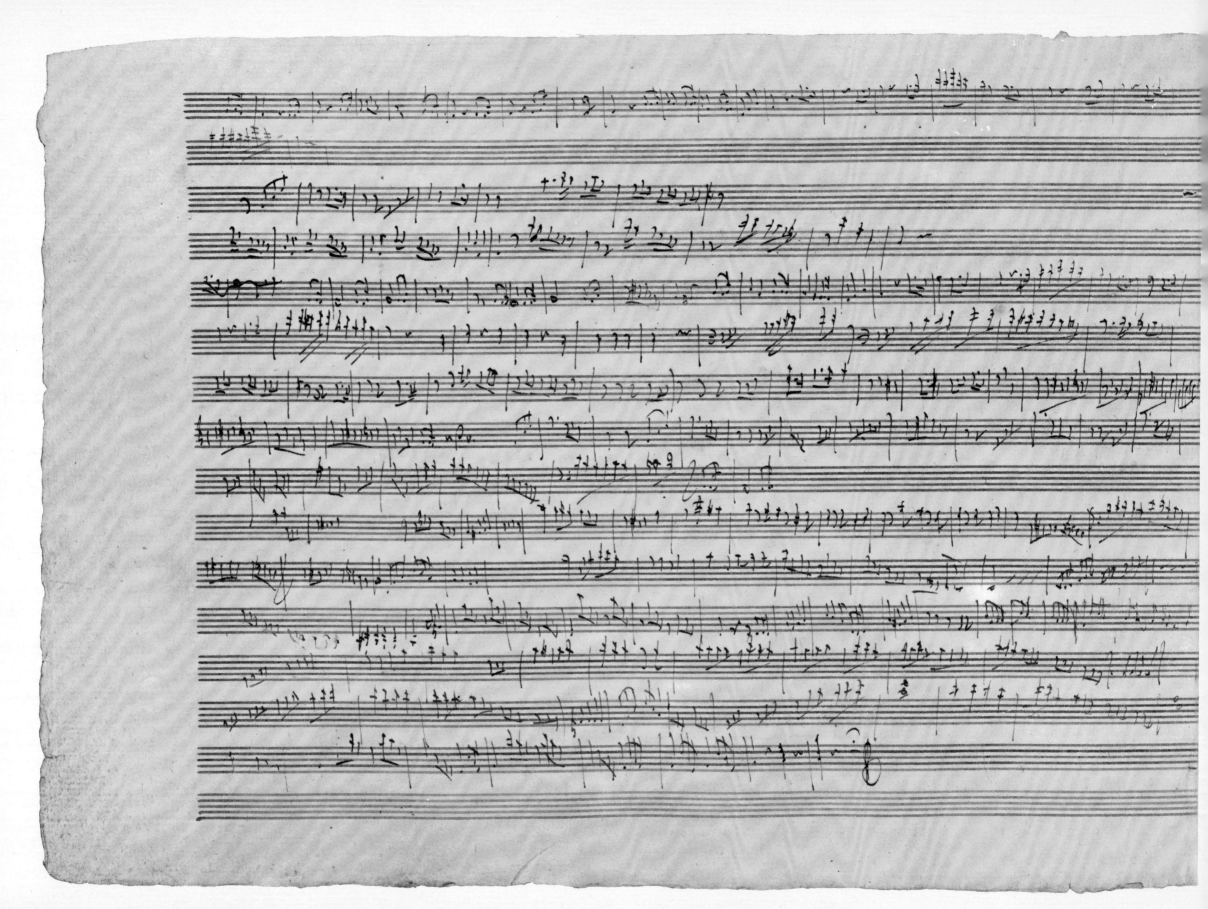

f. 106v

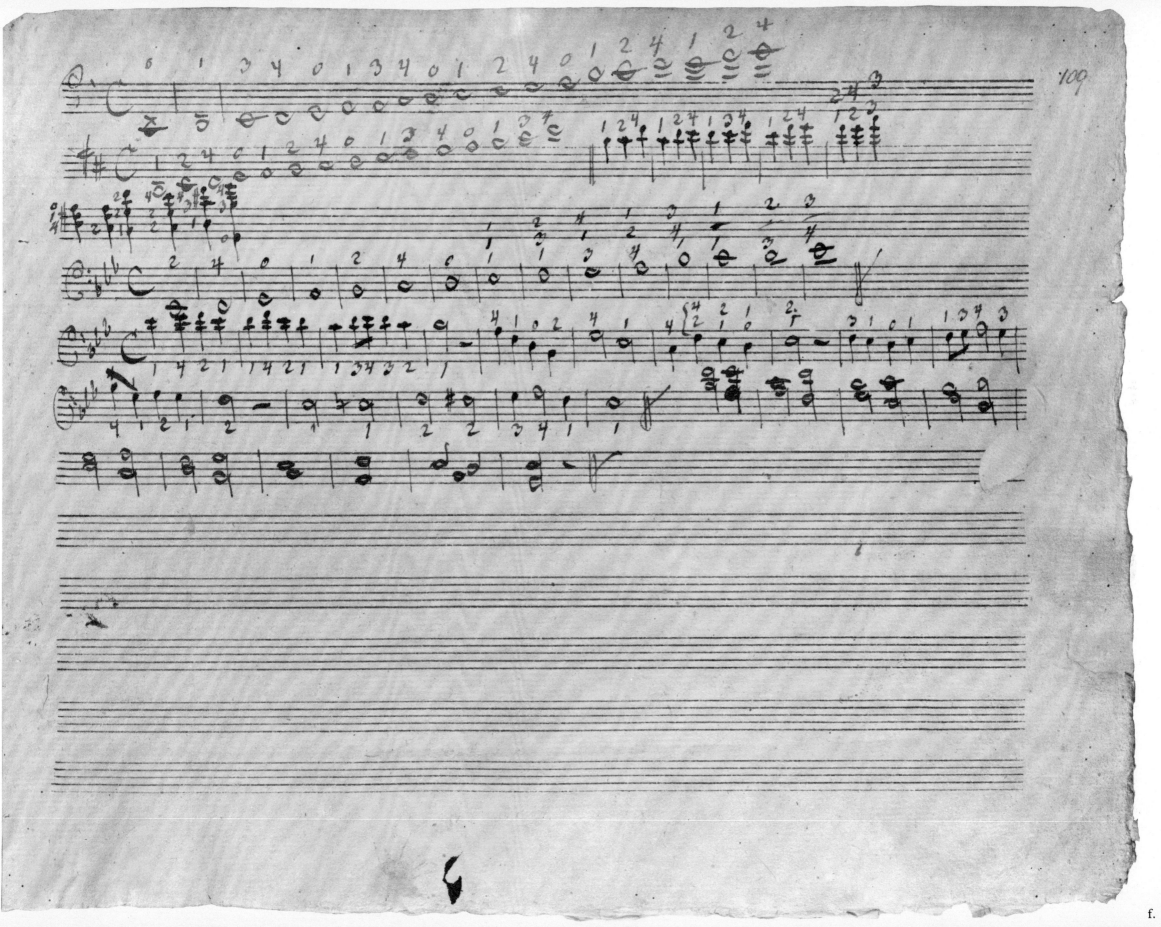

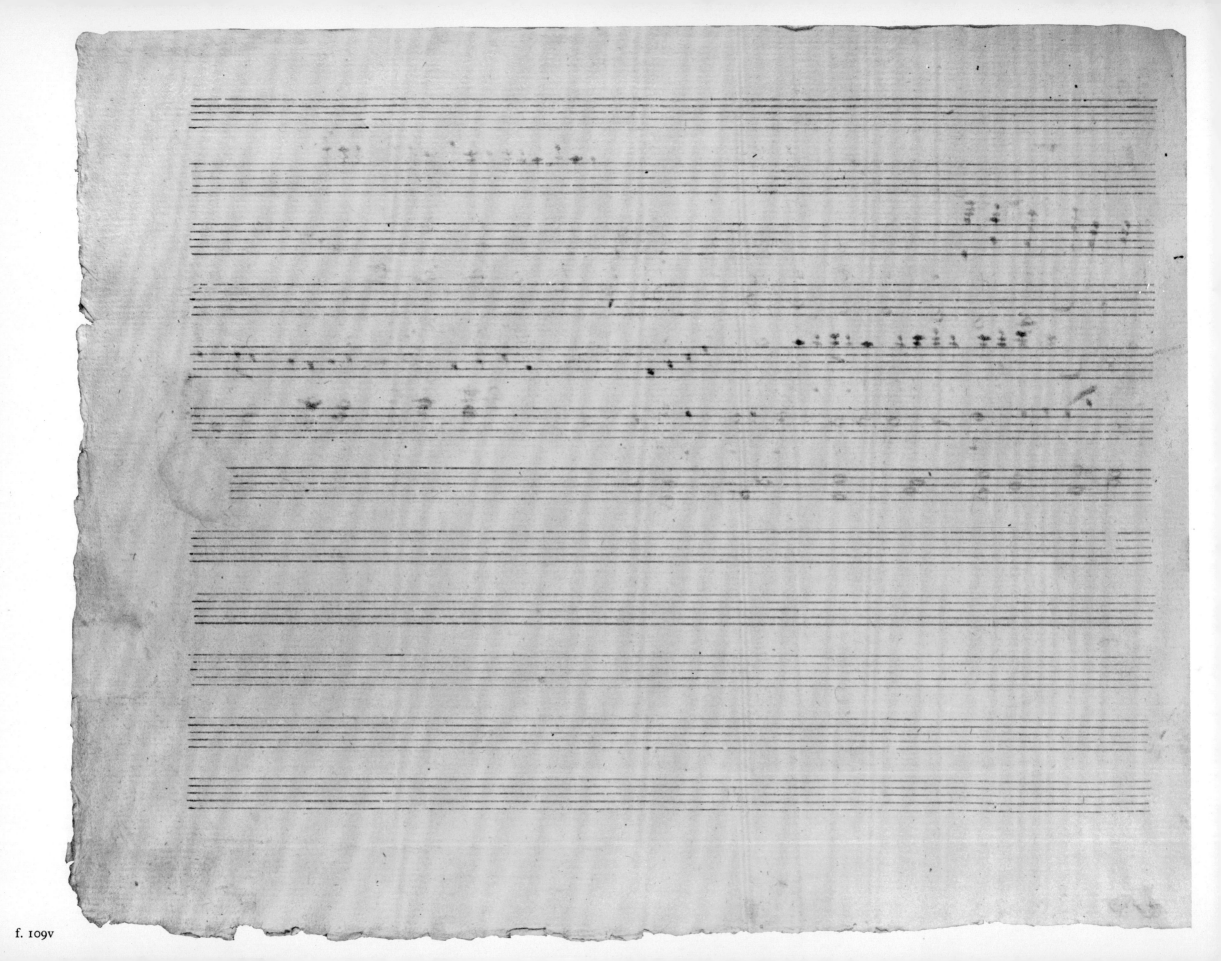

f. 109v

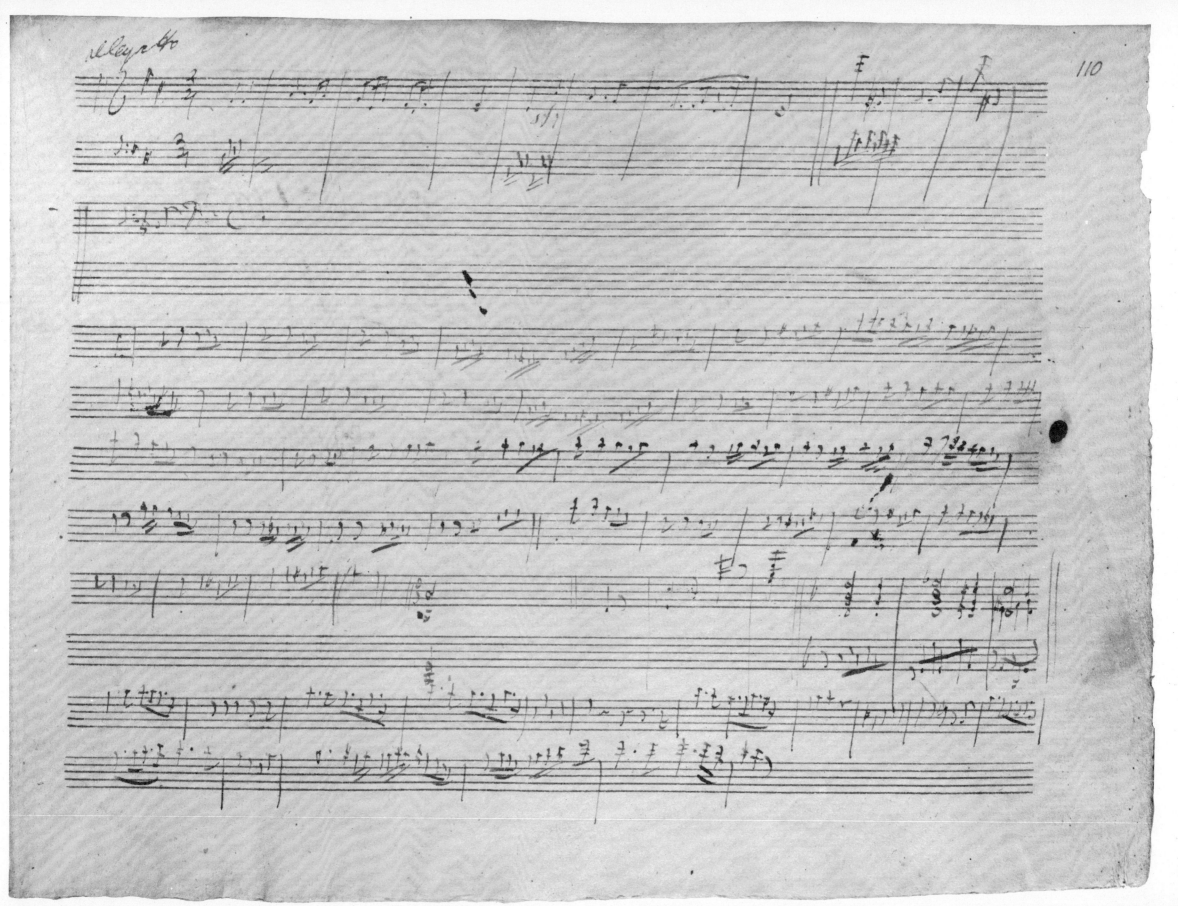

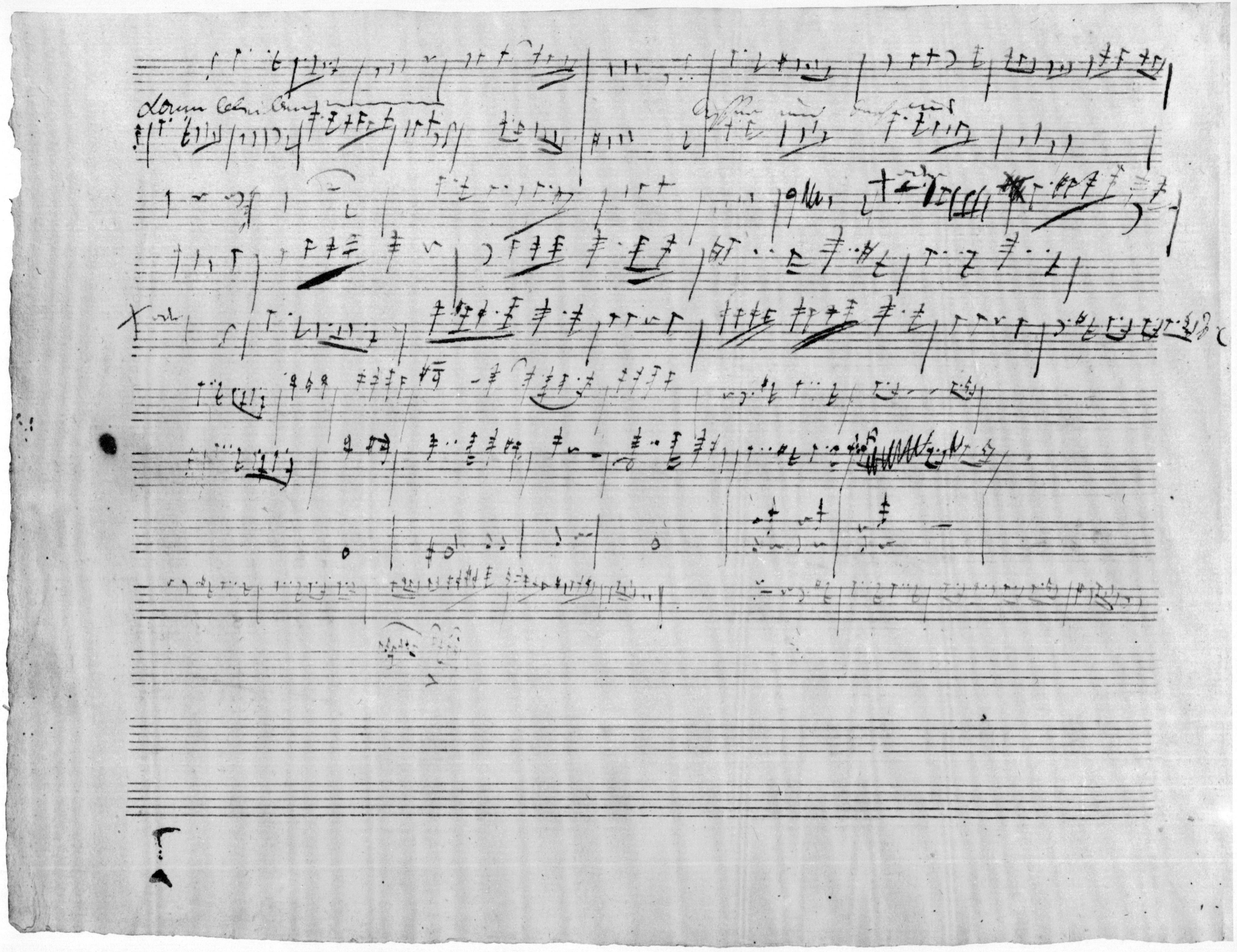

f. 110v

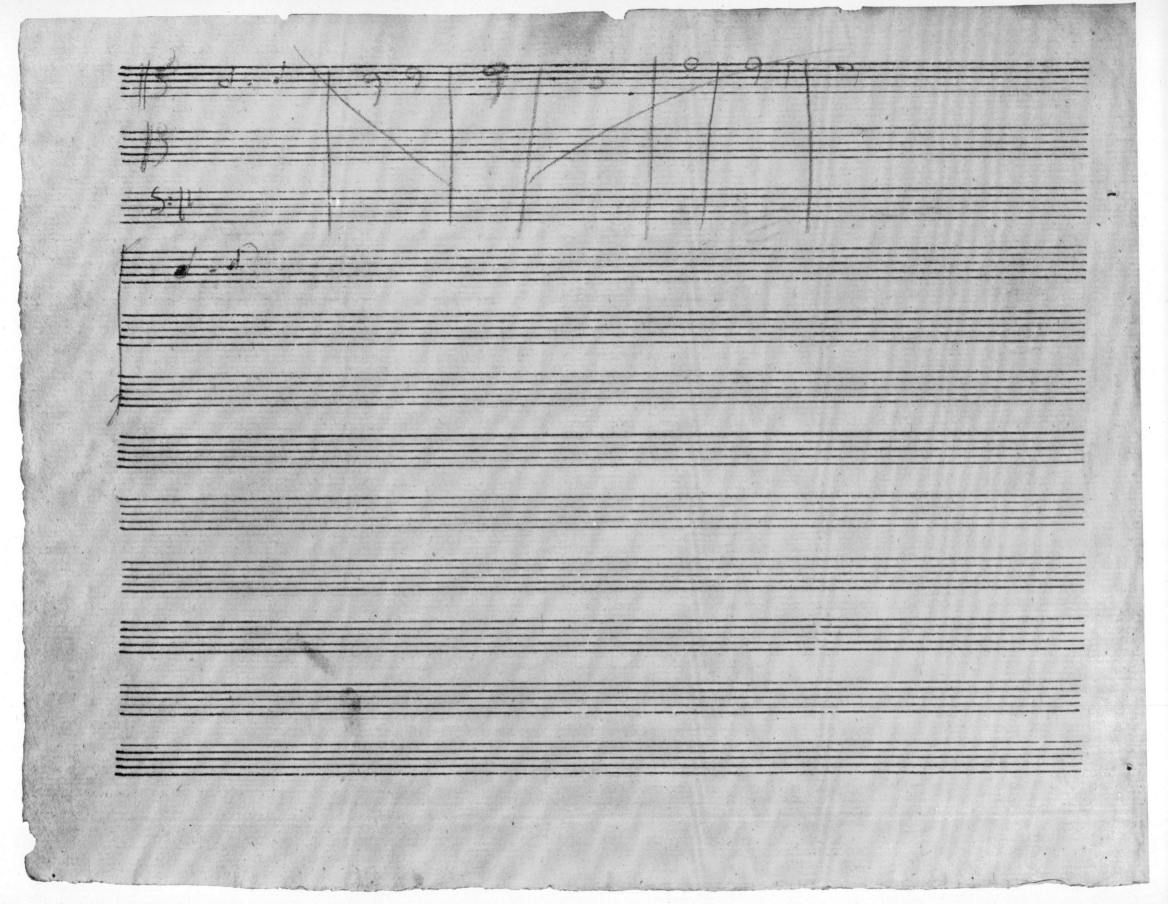

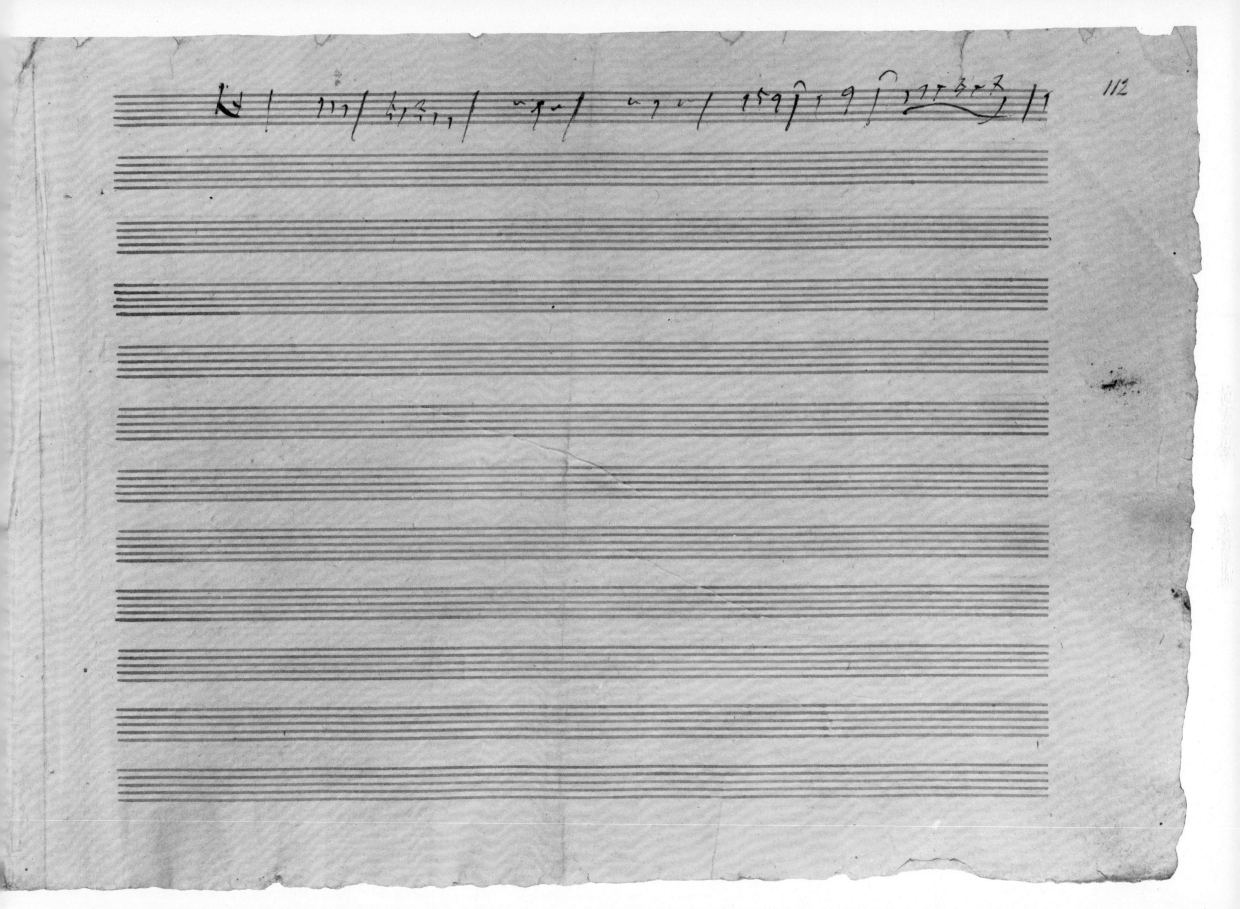

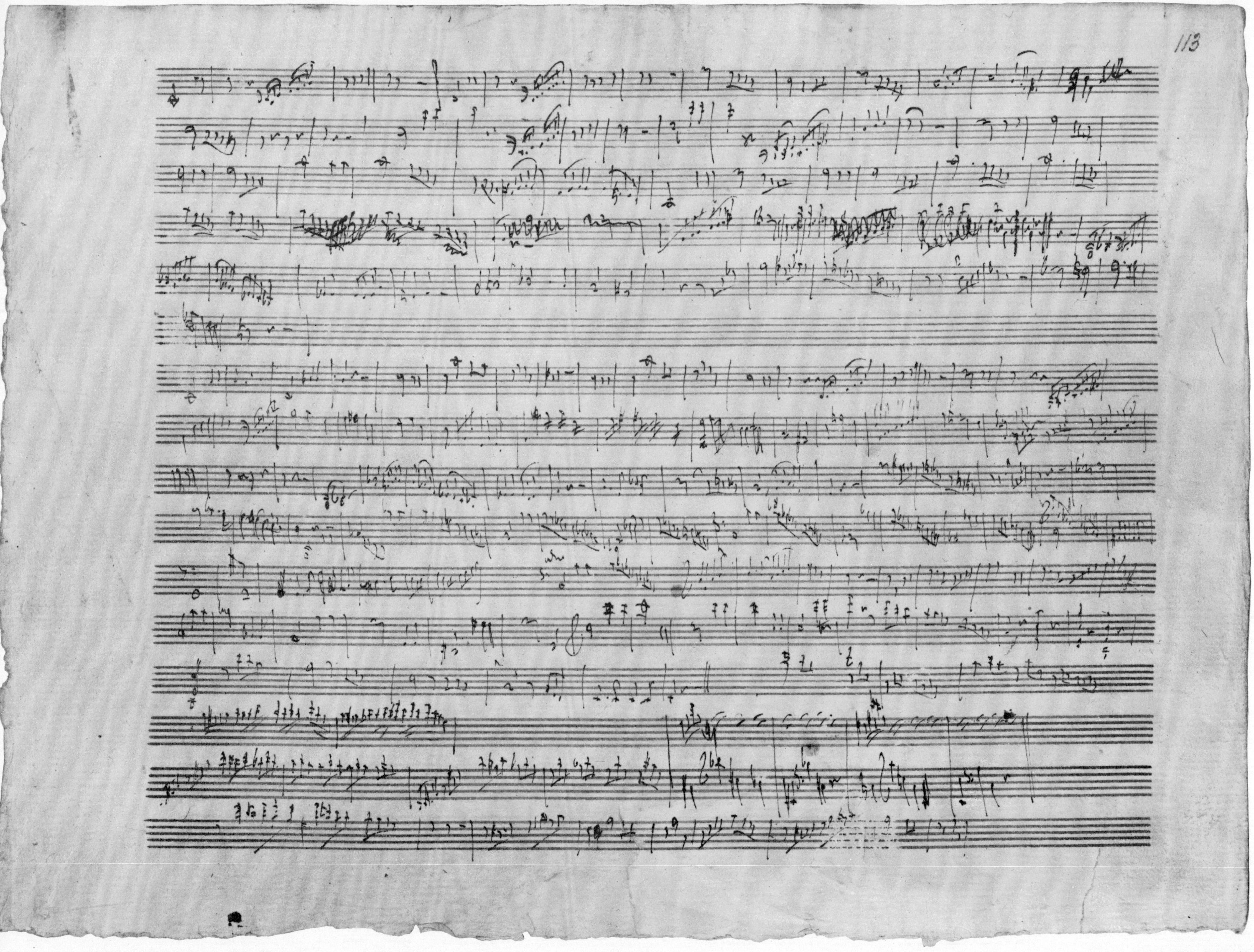

f. 113r

f. 114v

f. 115v

f. 116v

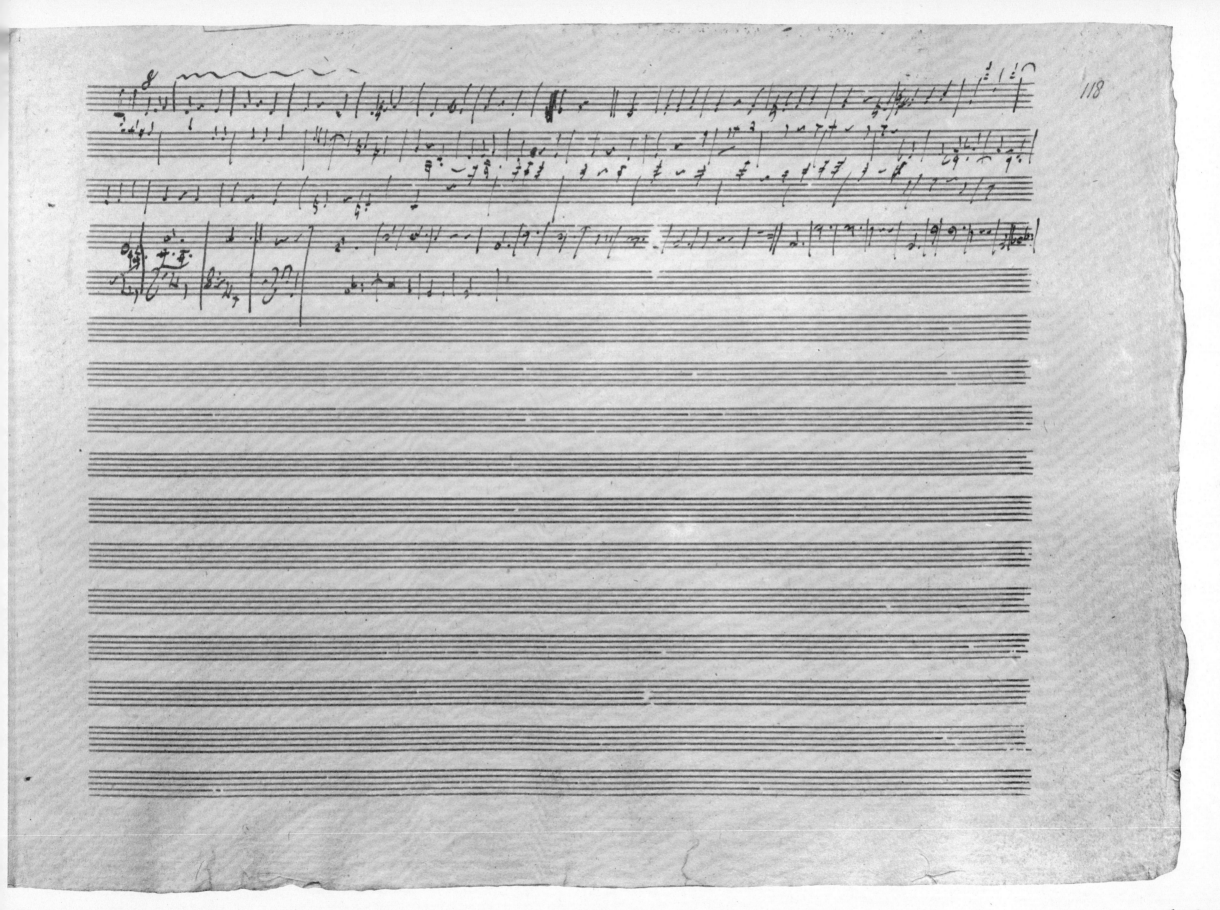

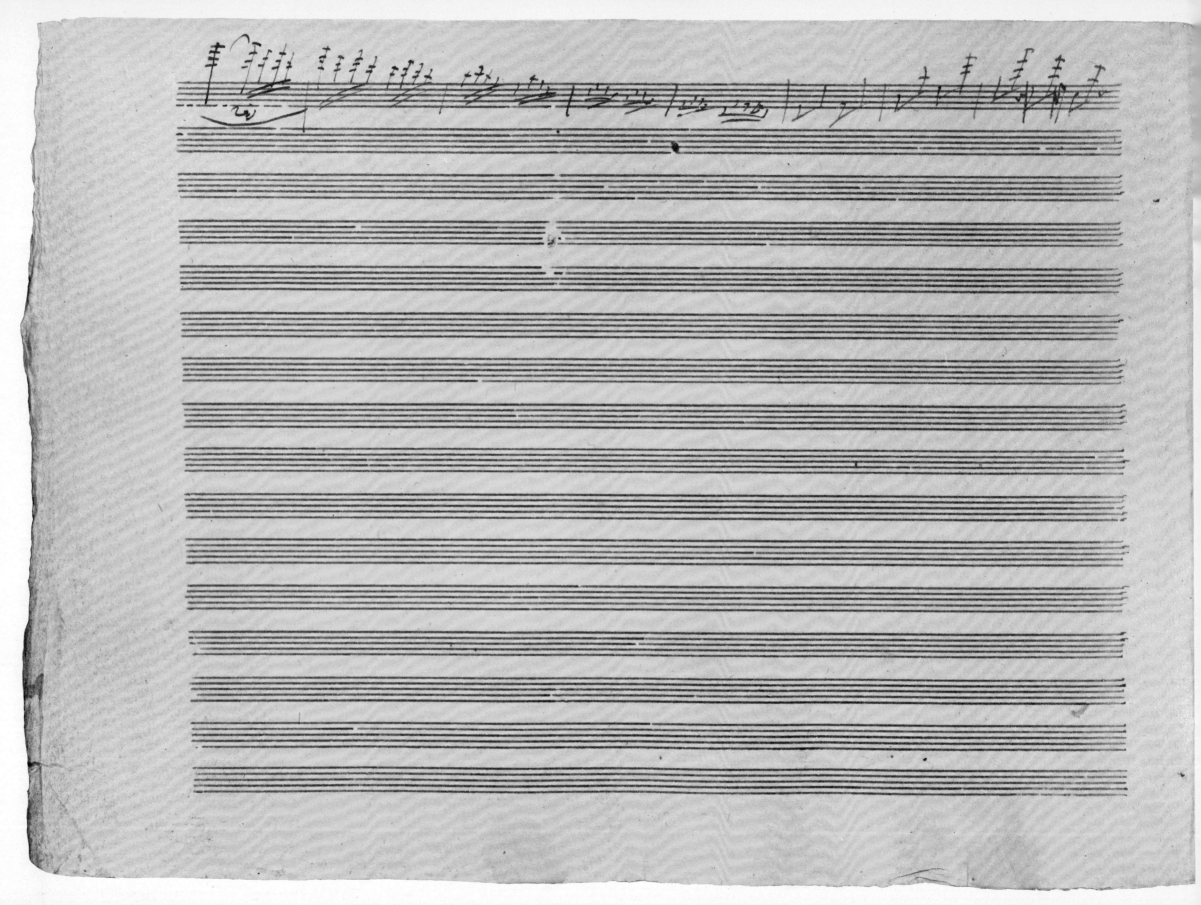

f. 119v

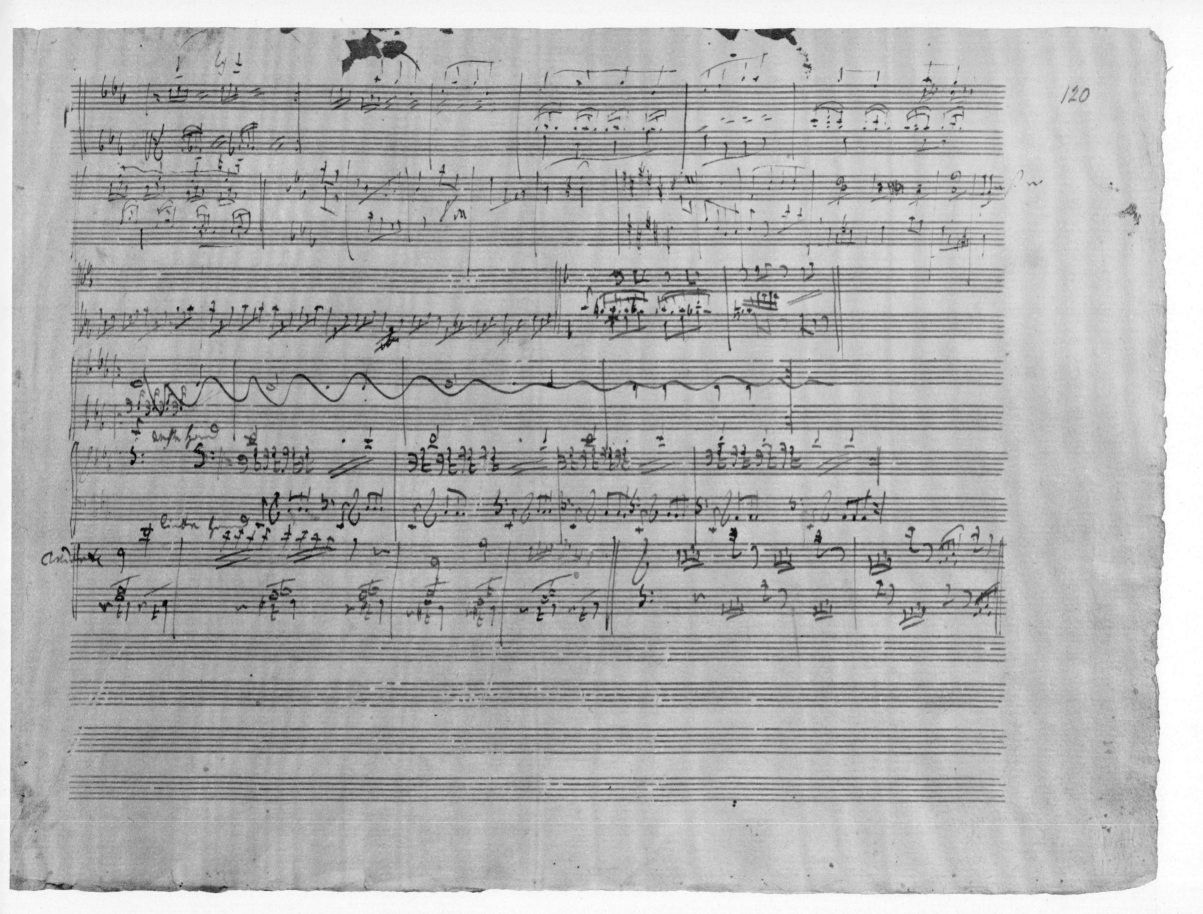

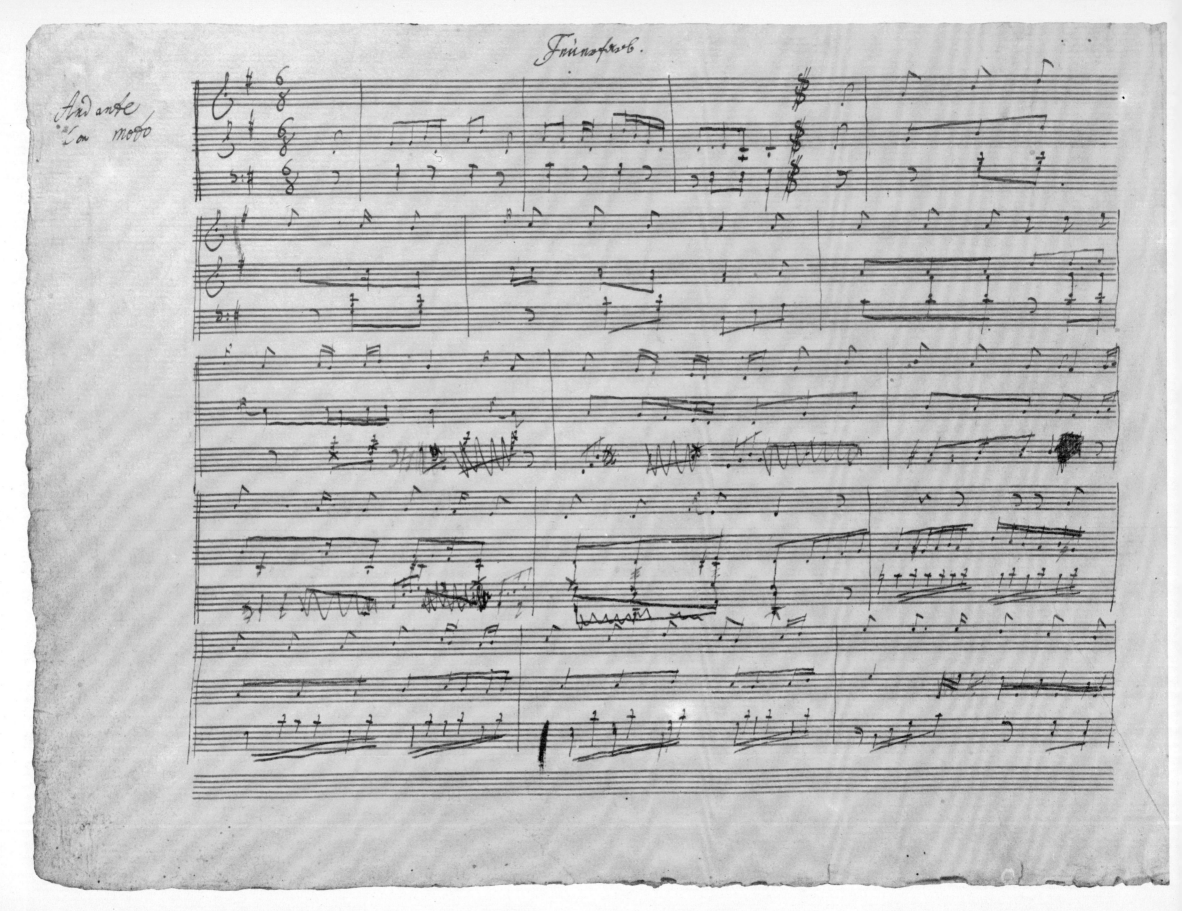

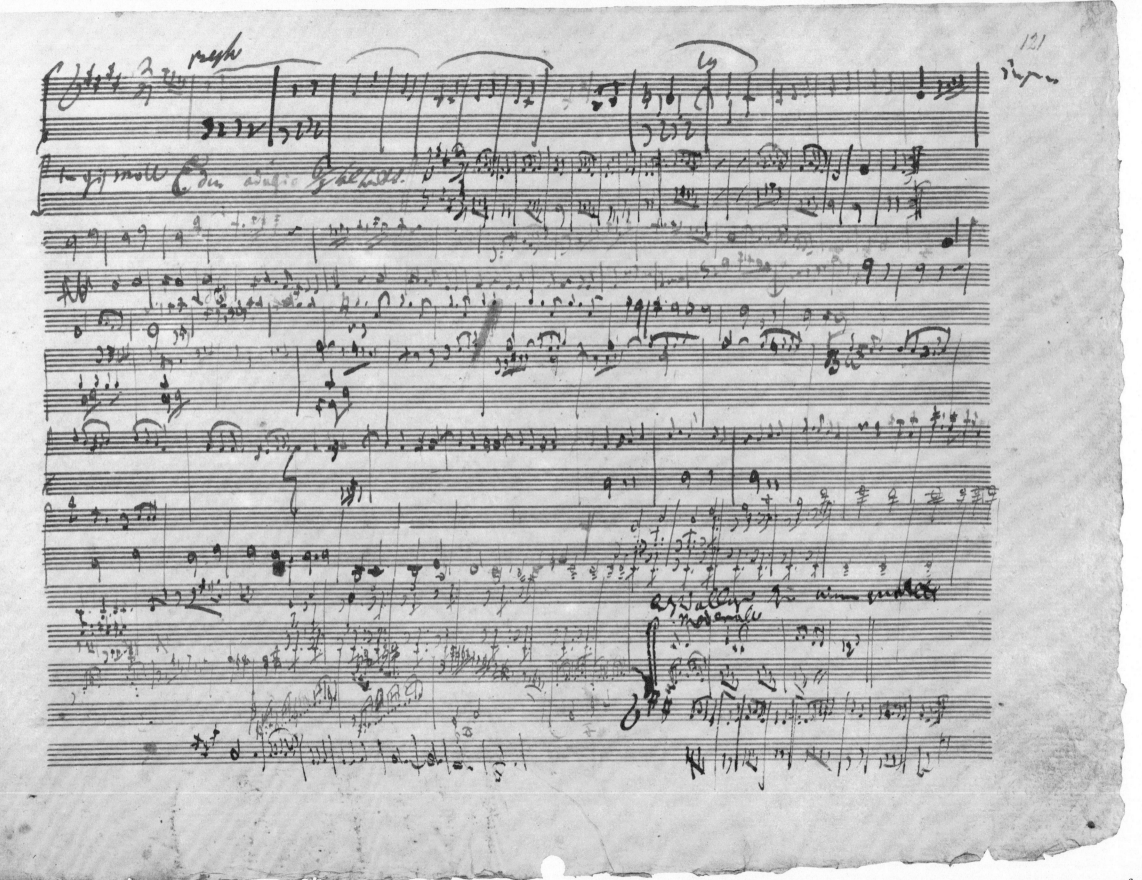

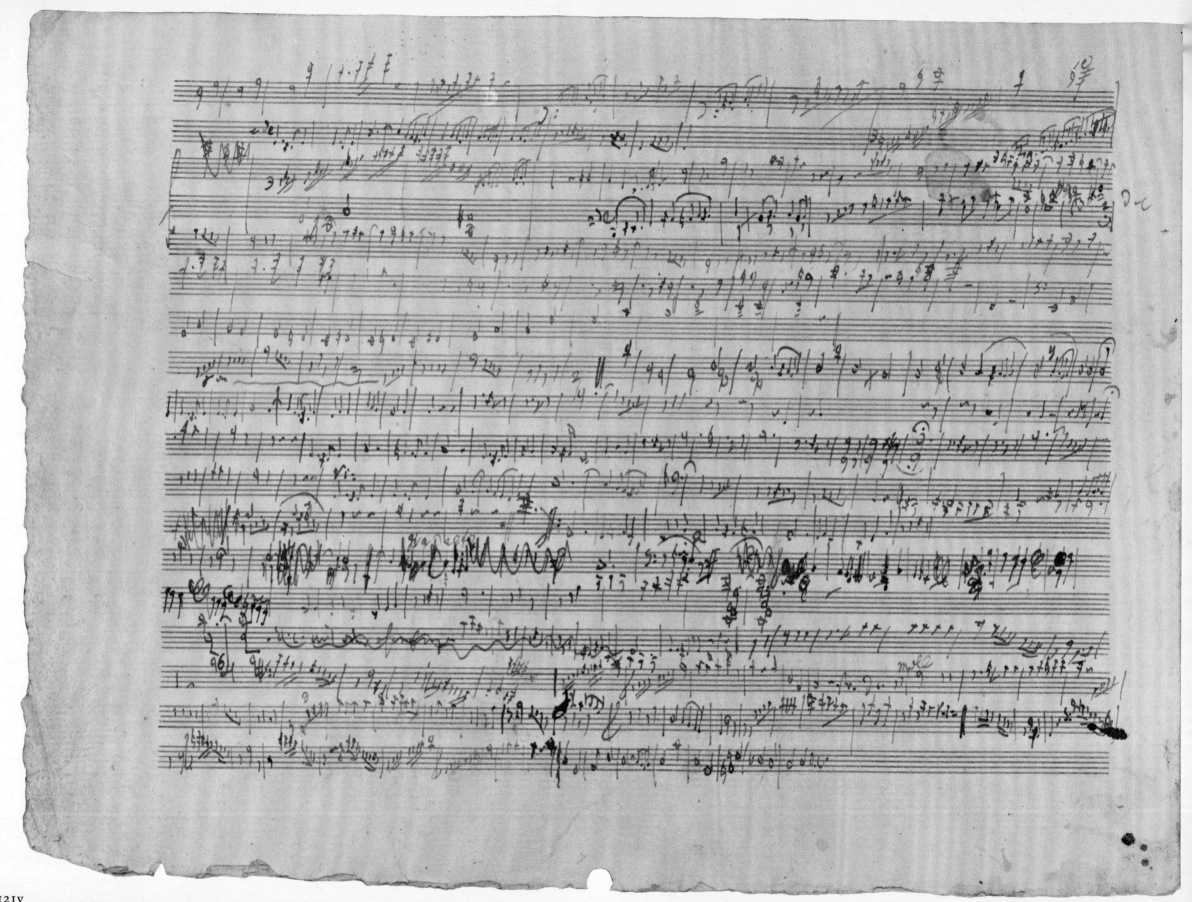

f. 121ᵛ

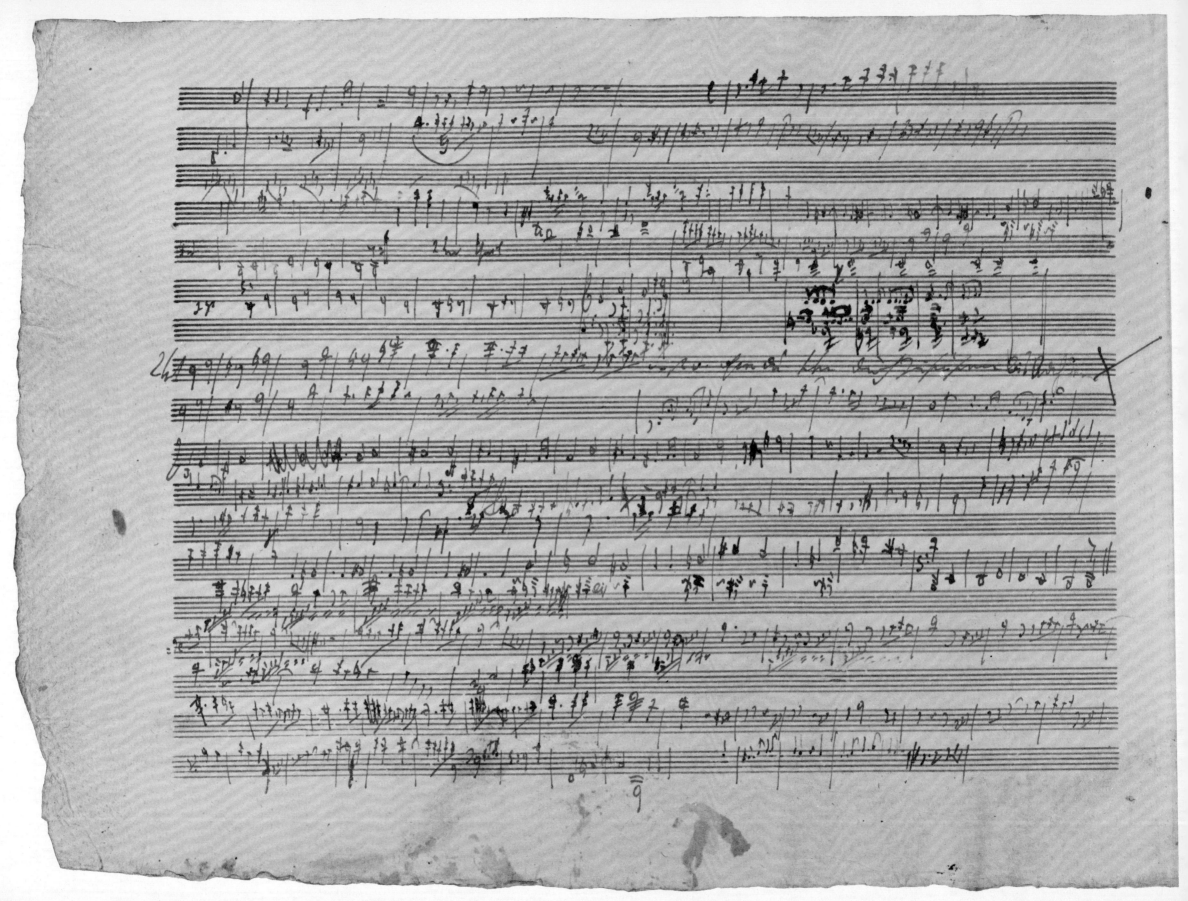

f. 123r

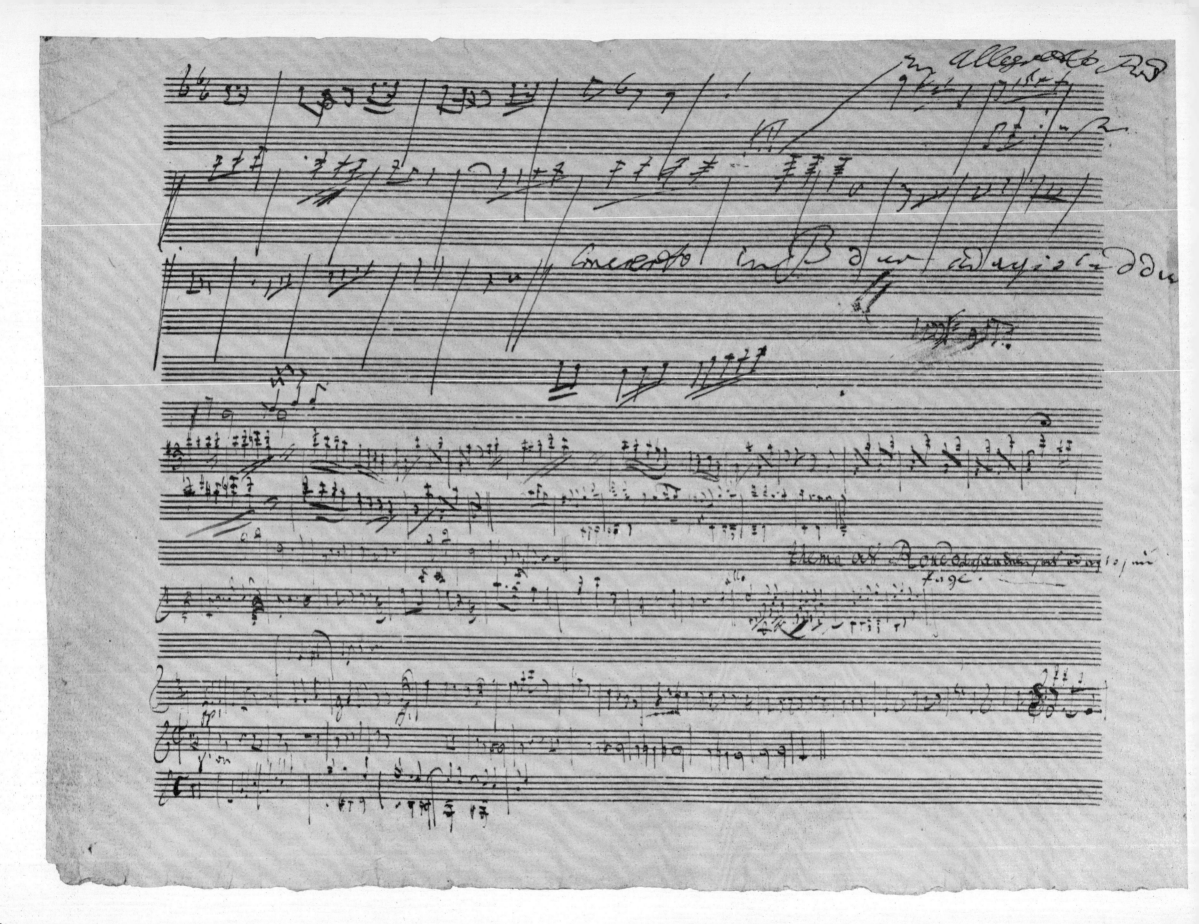

f. 127v

f. 128v

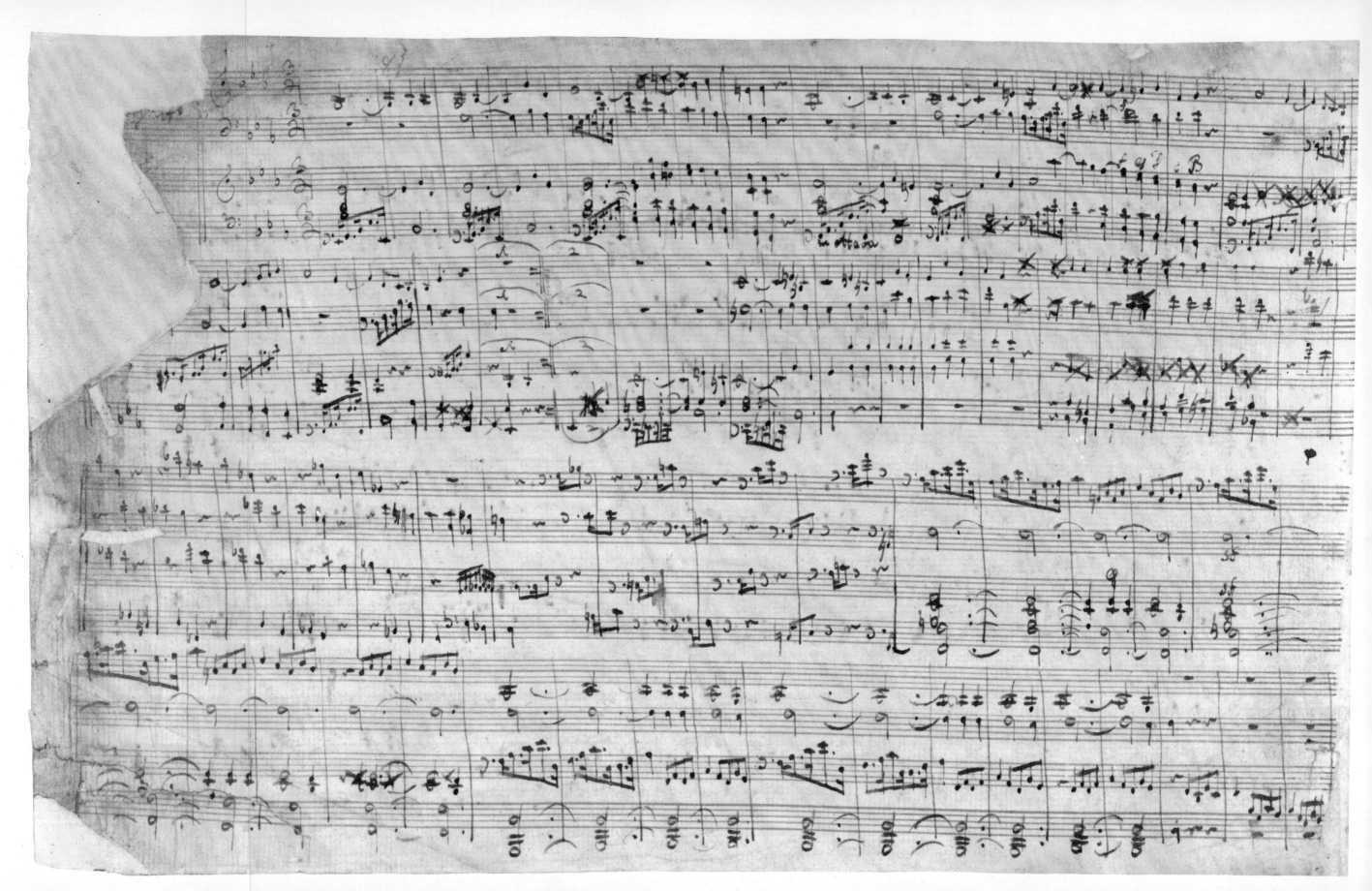

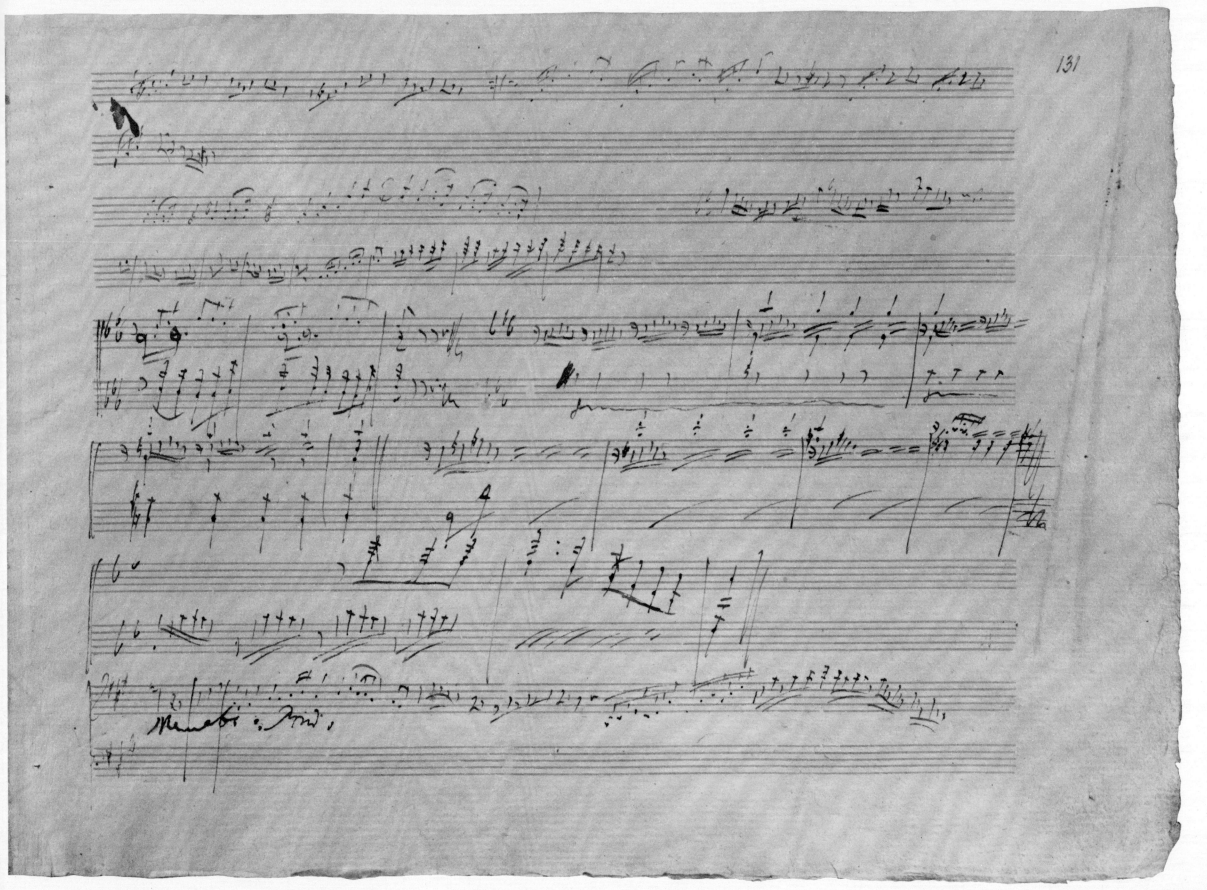

f. 132v

133

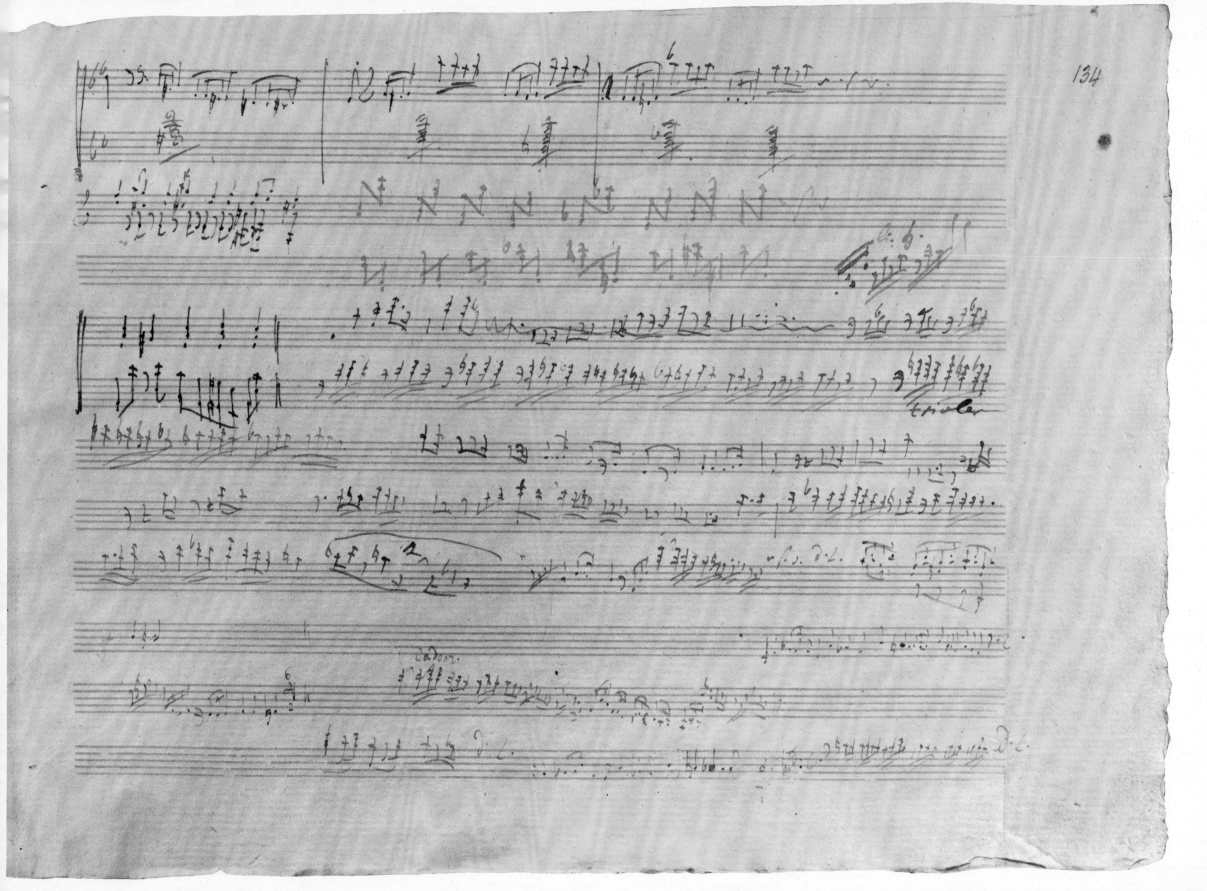

f. 136v

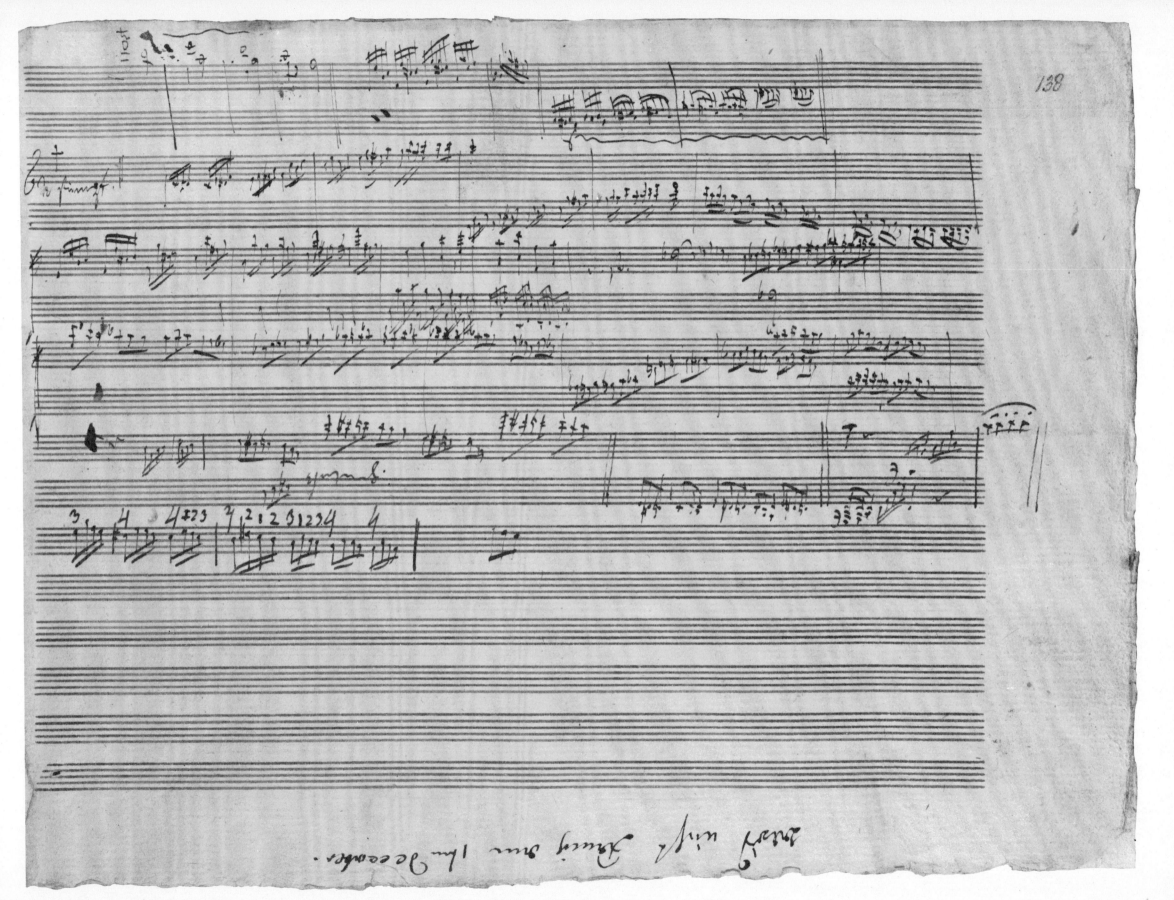

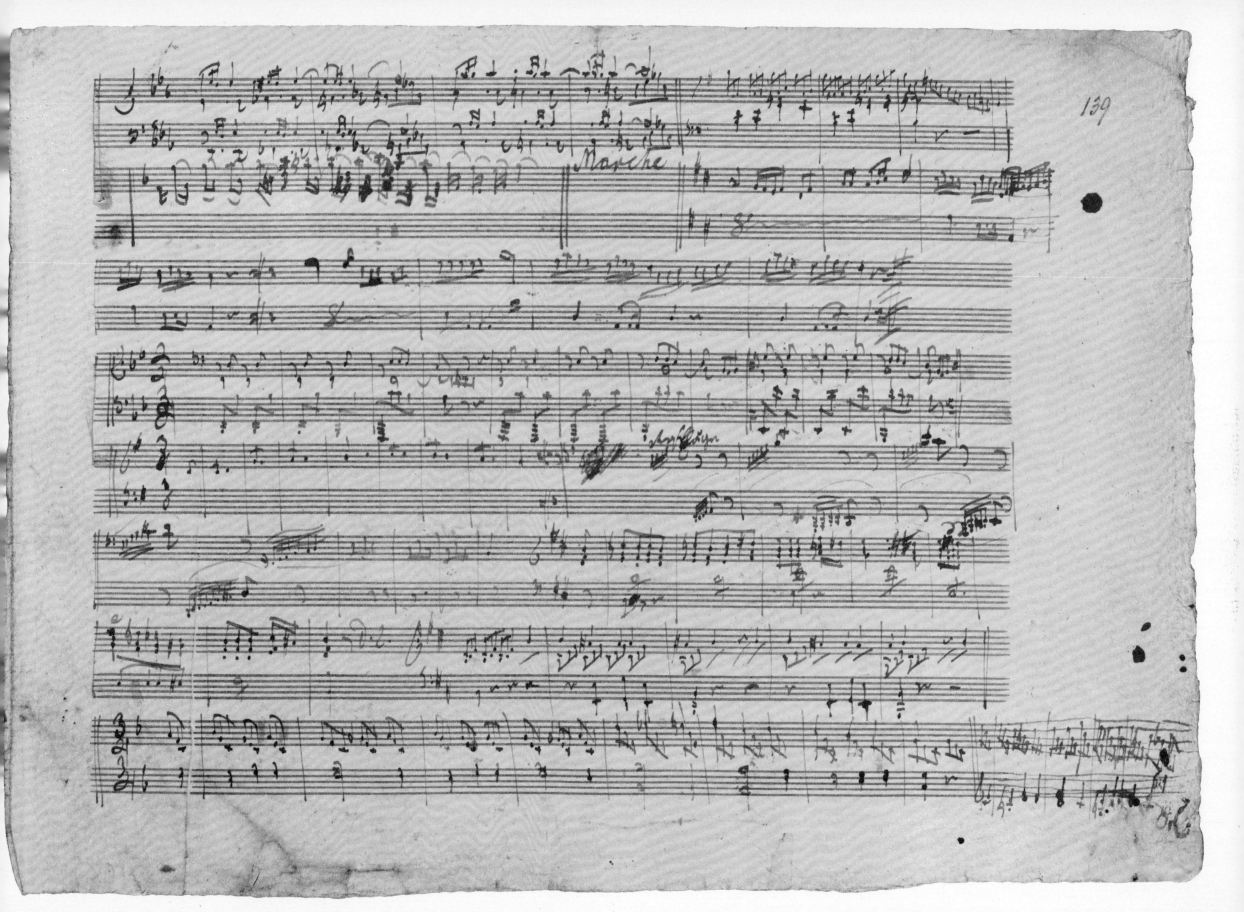

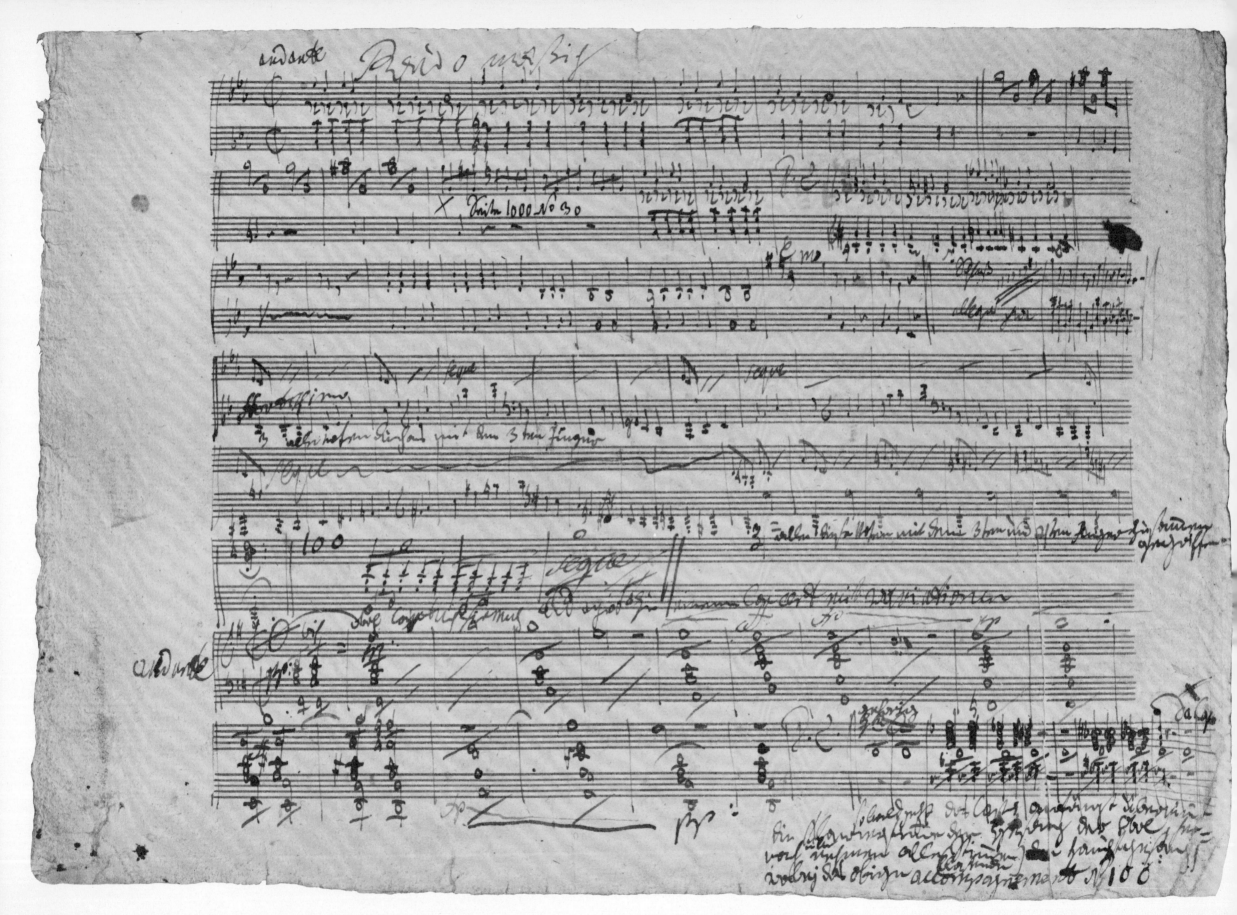

f. 139v

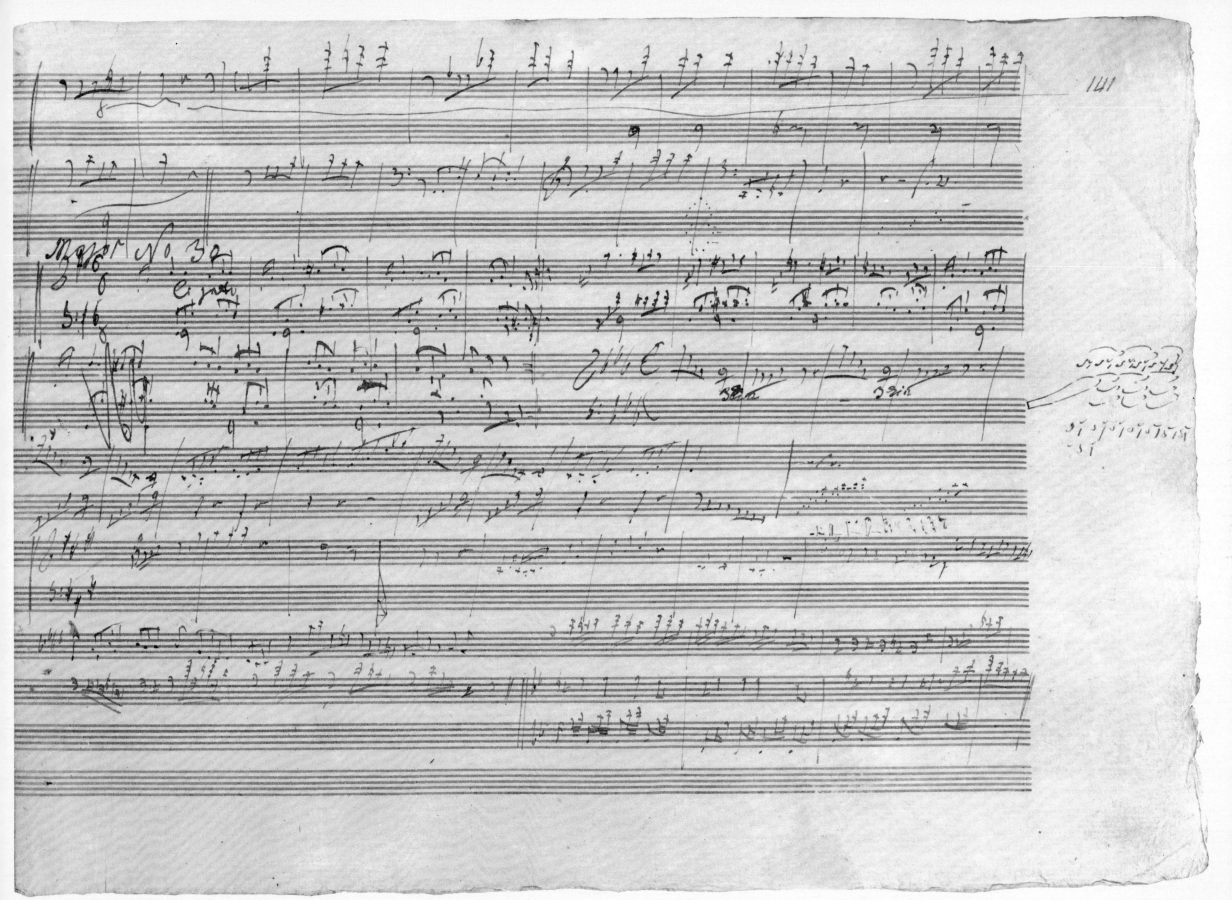

f. 141v

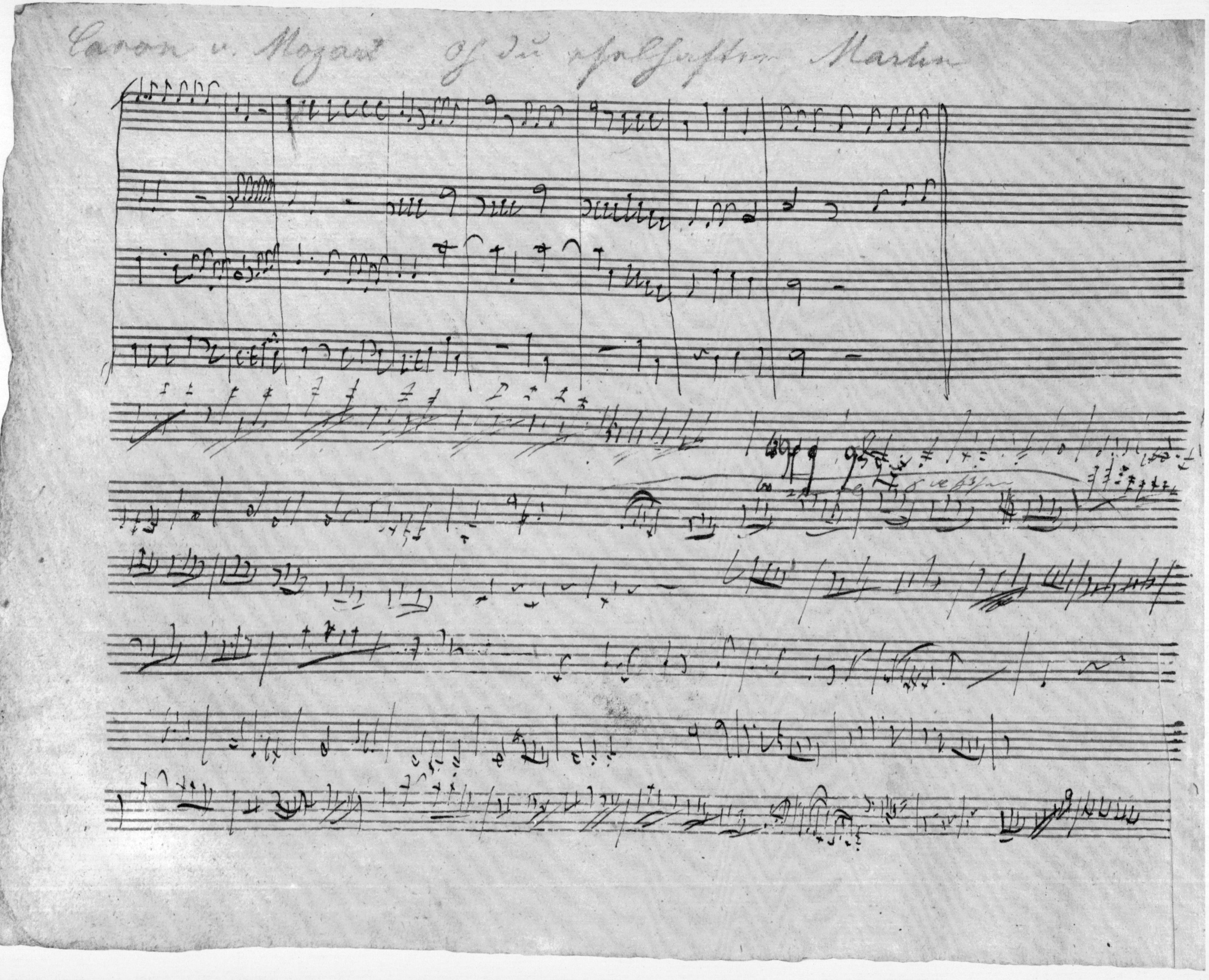

f. 142v

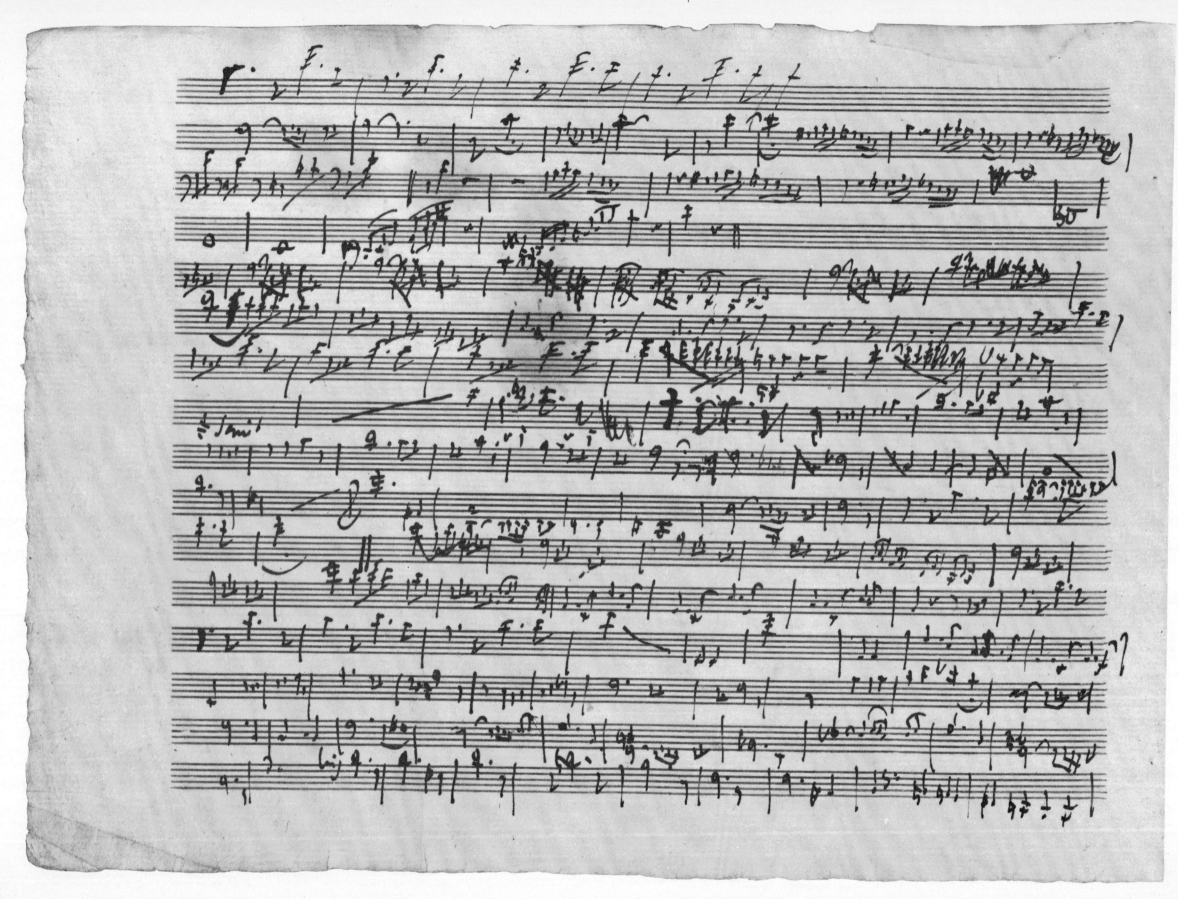

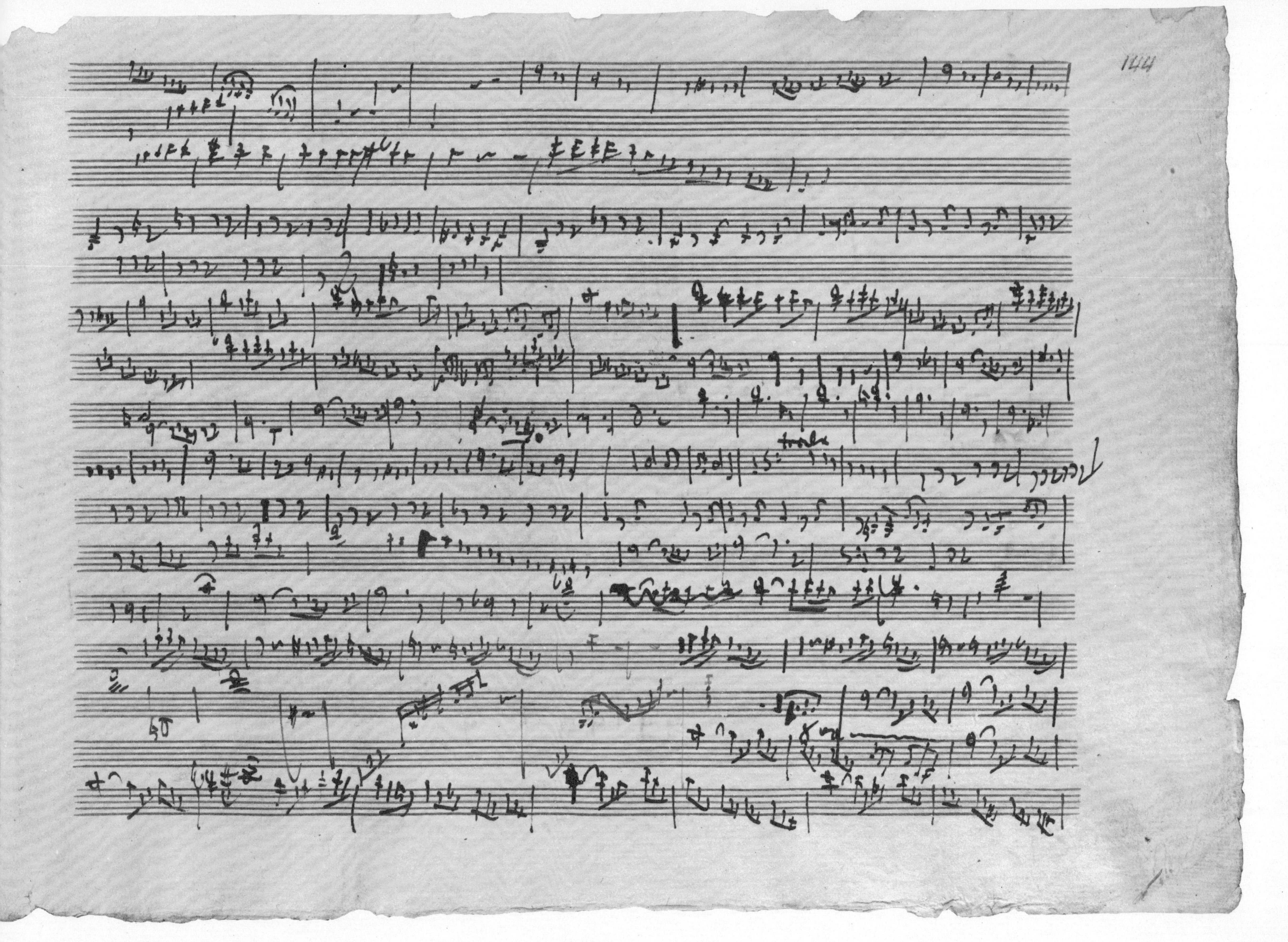

f. 144r

f. 144v

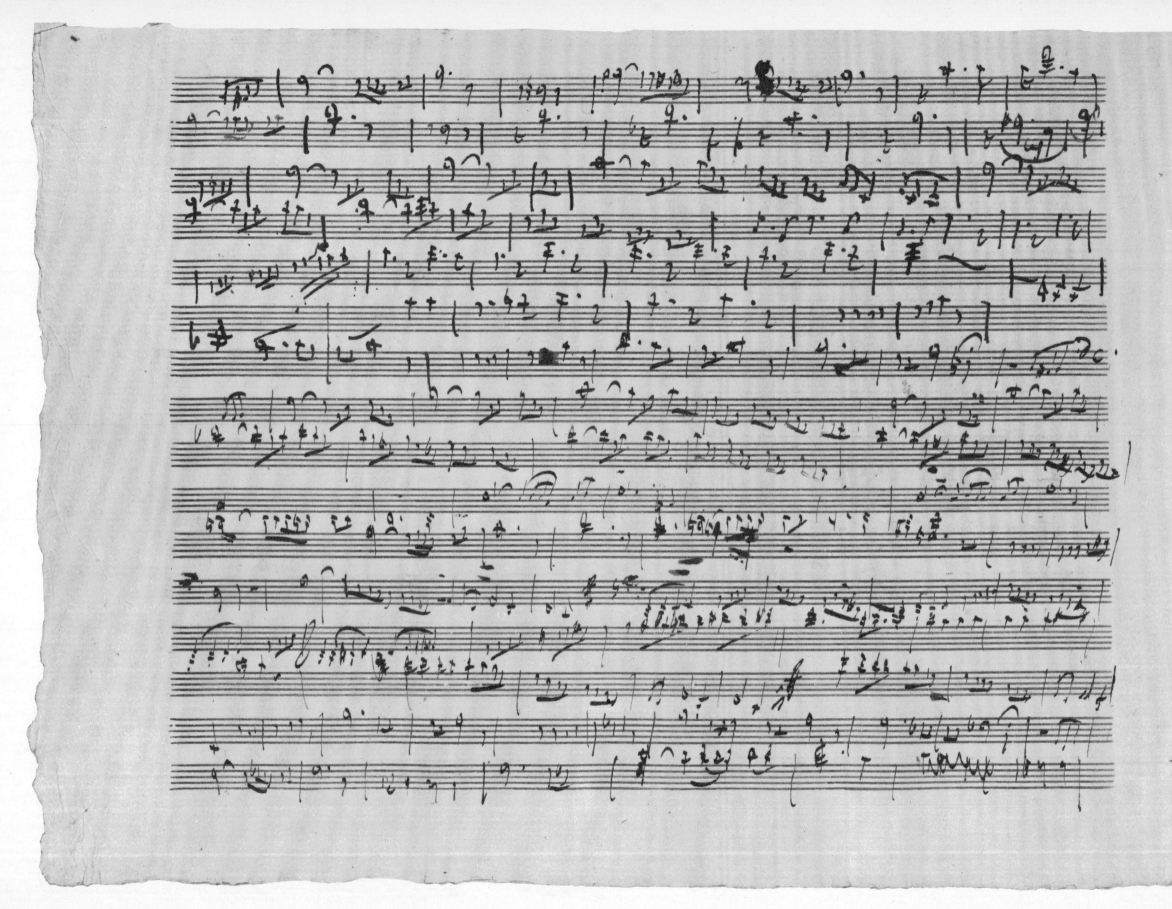

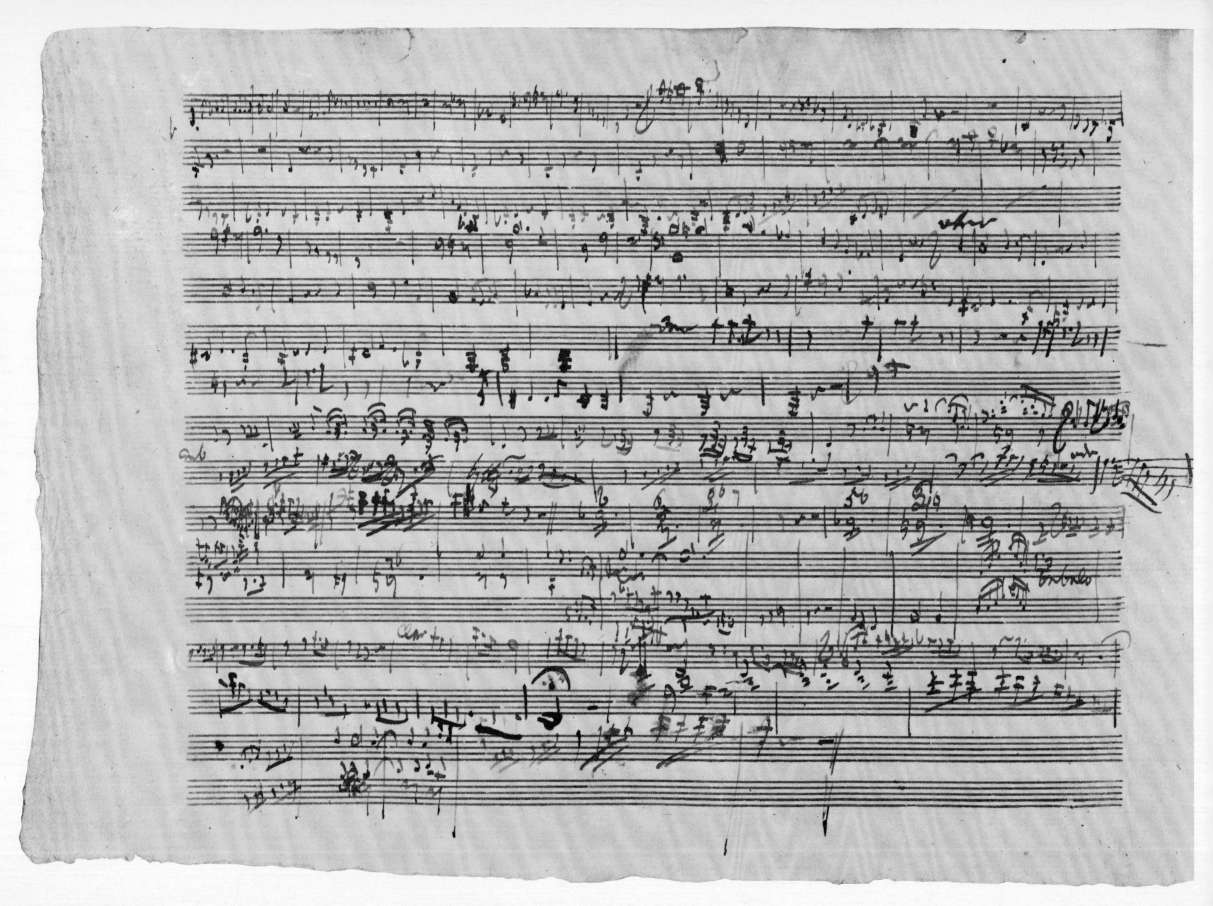

f. 146v

f. 147v

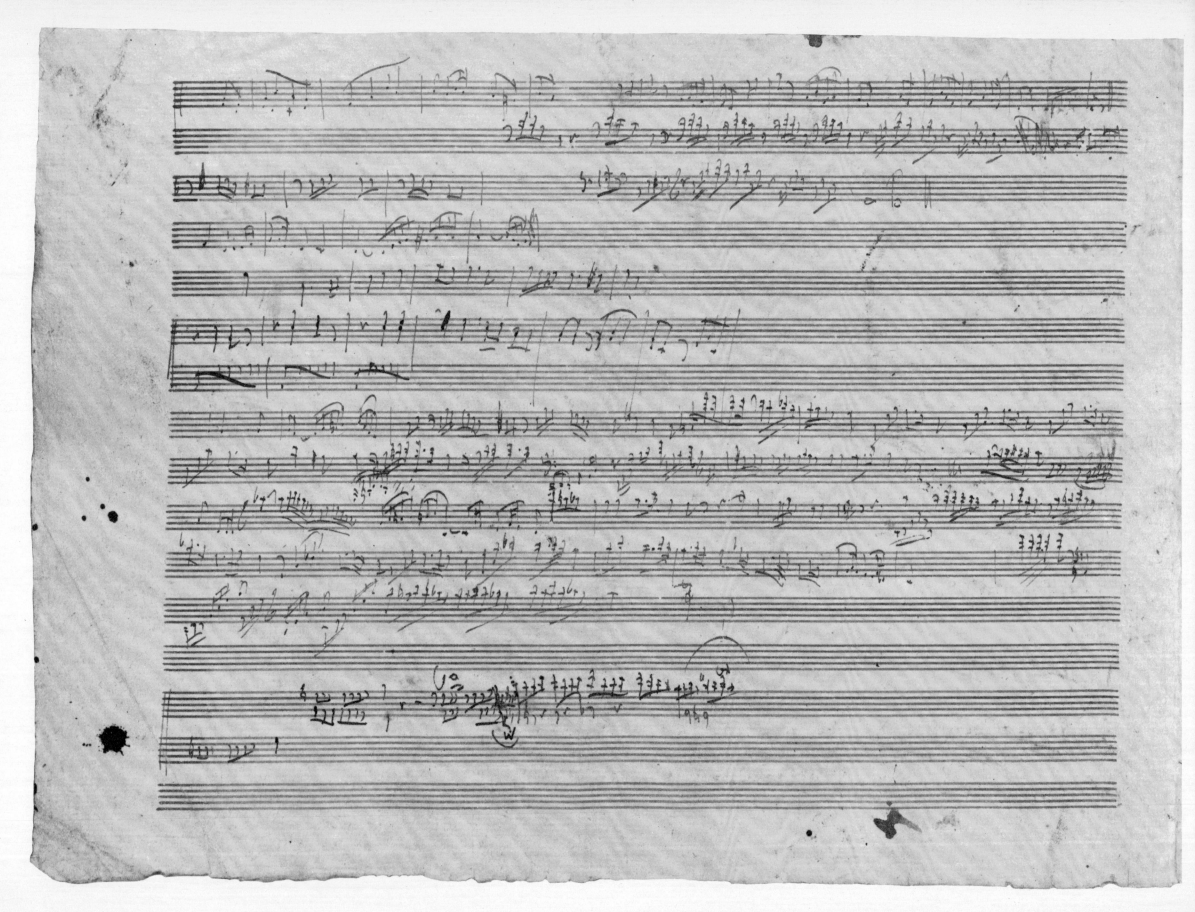

f. 149v

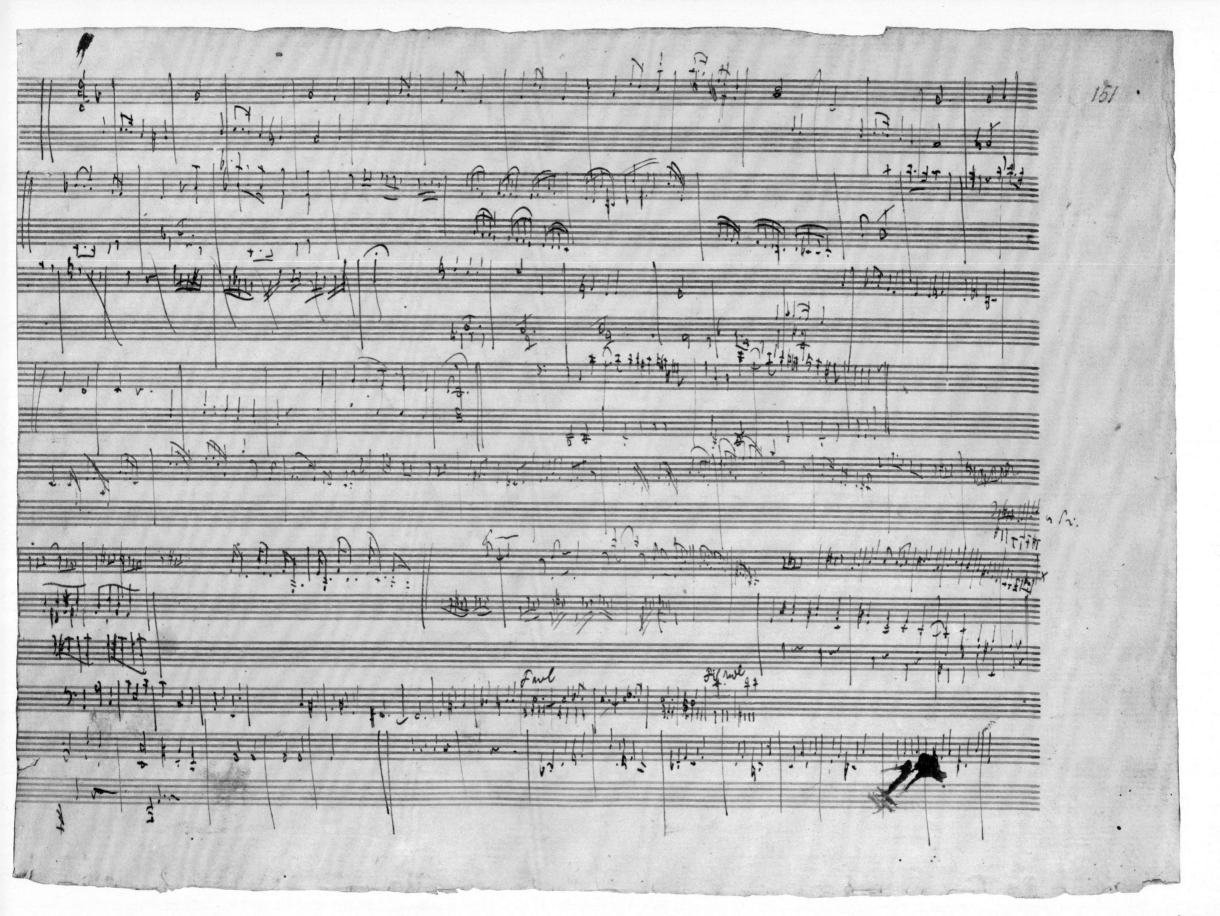

f. 151r

f. 151v

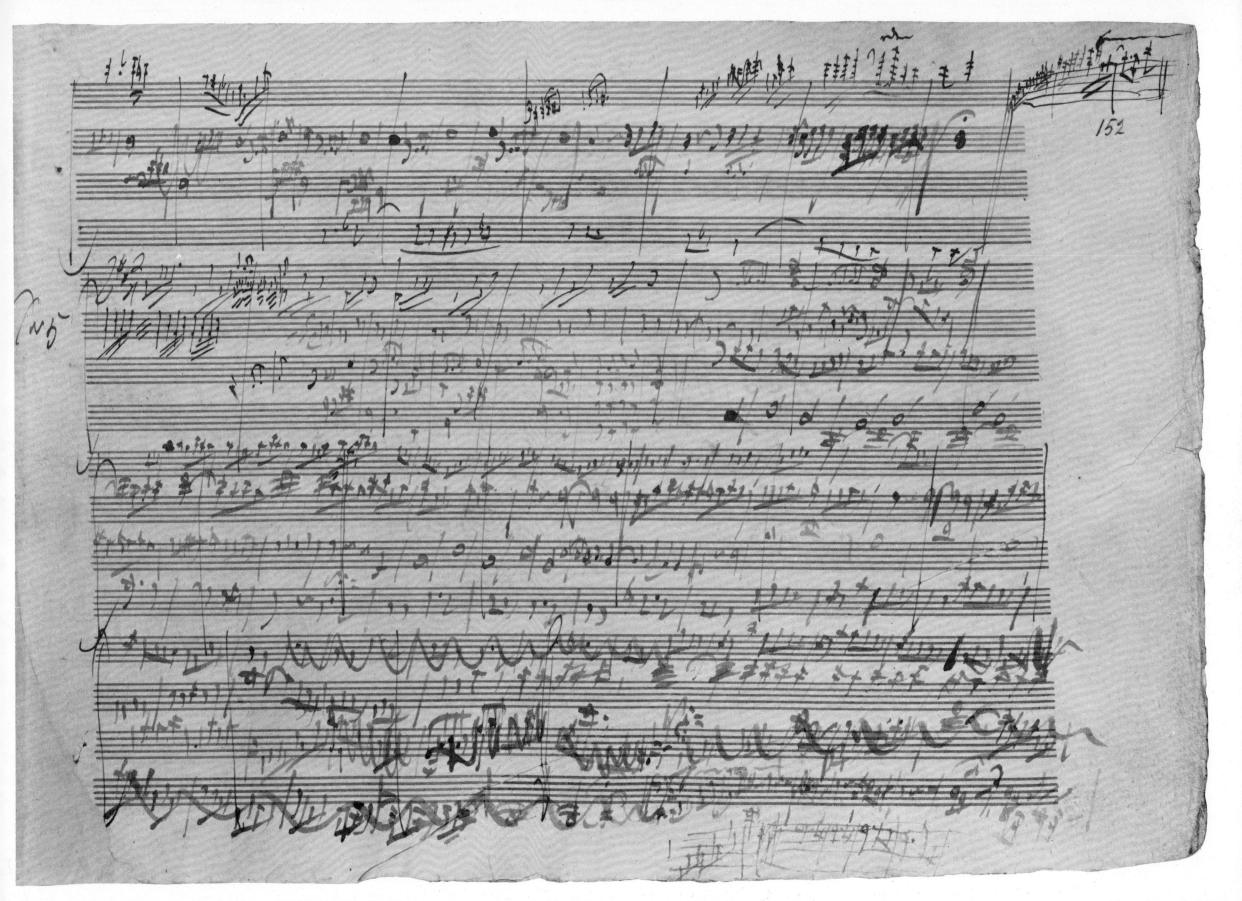

f. 152v

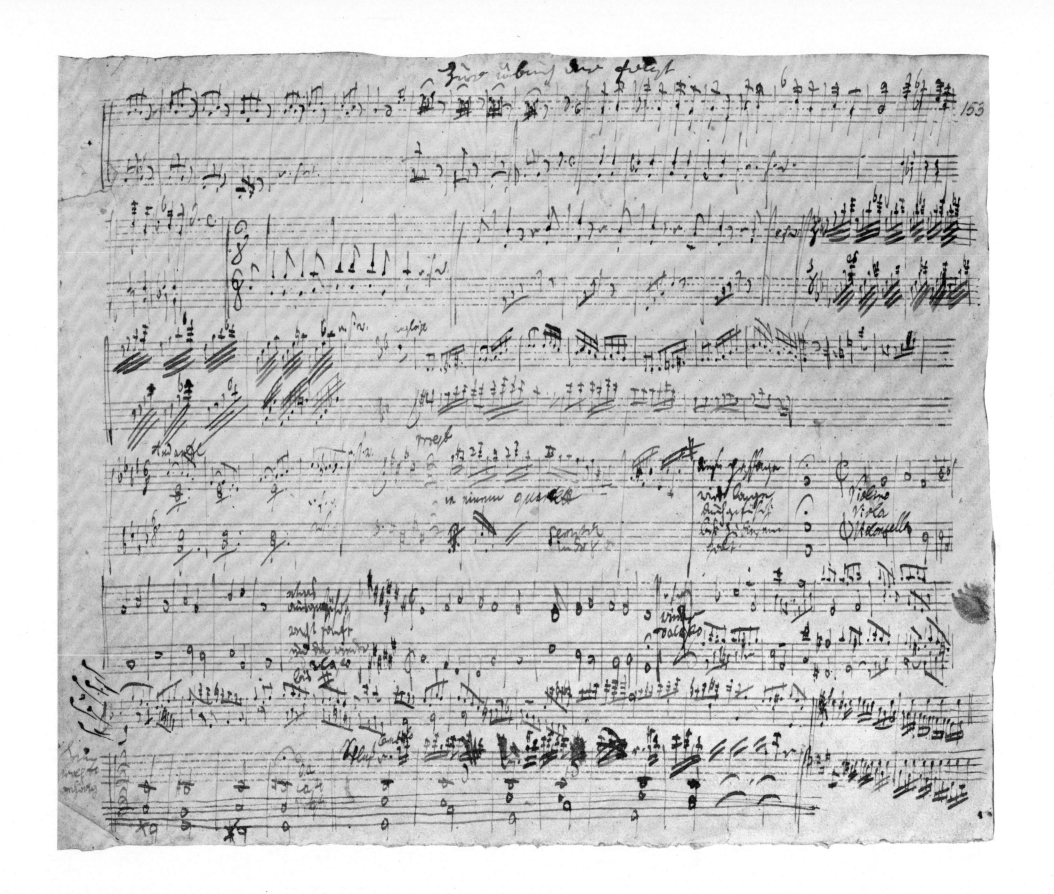

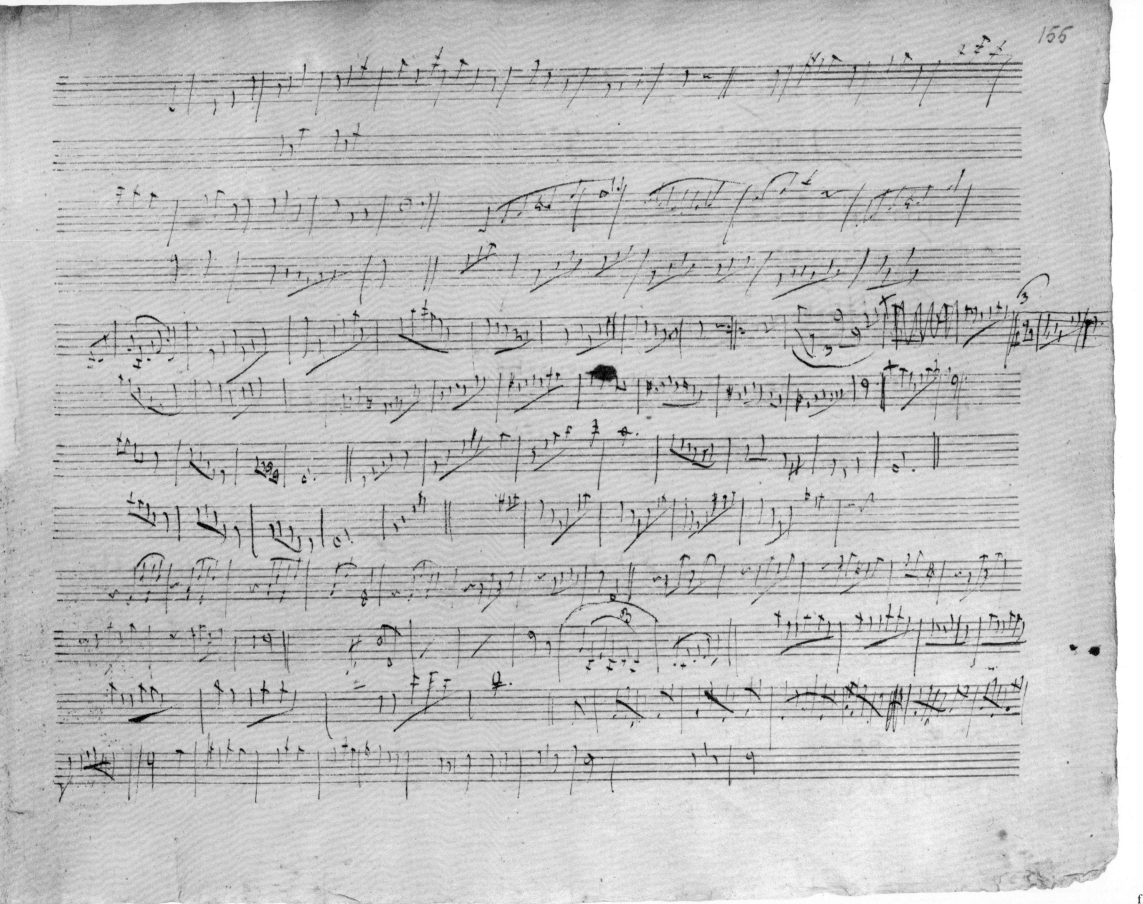

f. 155v

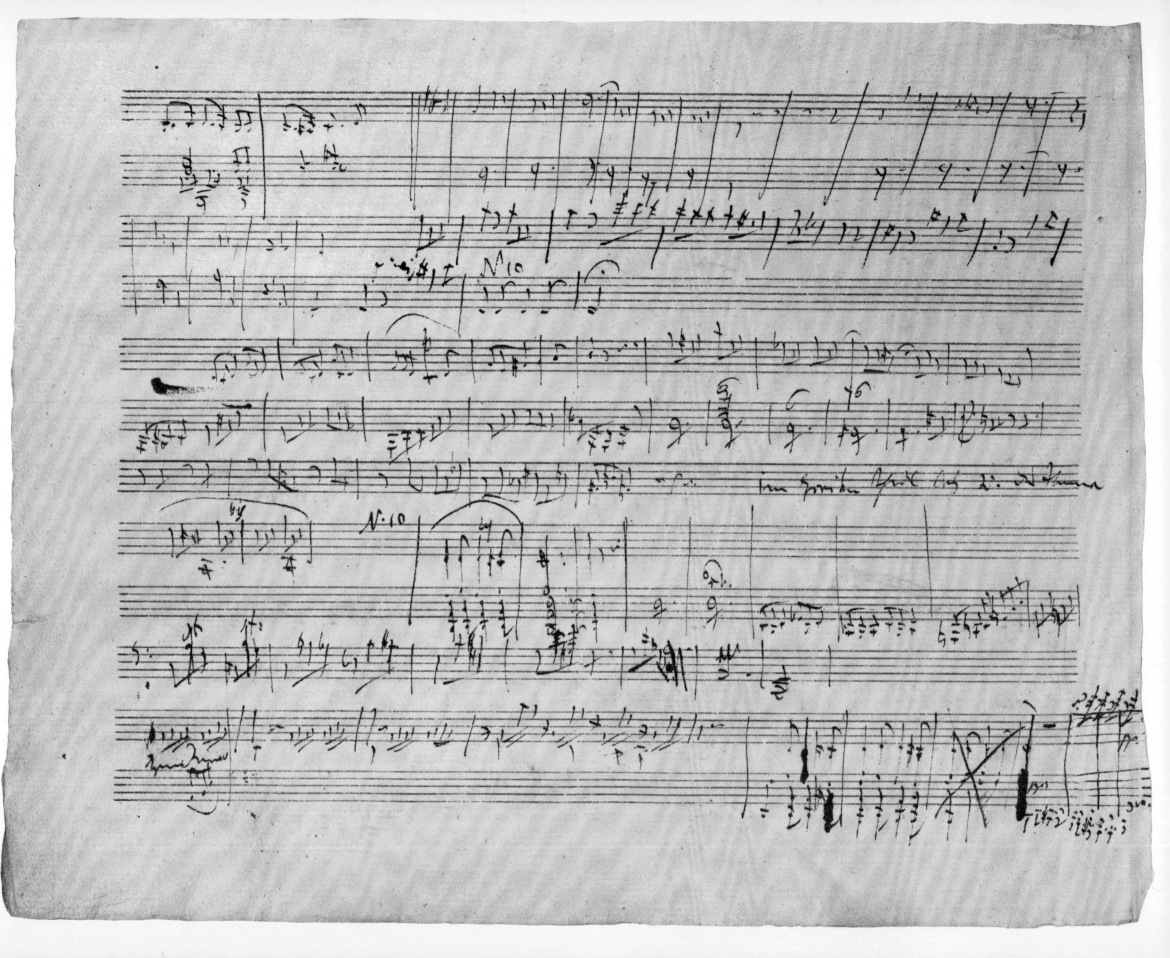

f. 156v

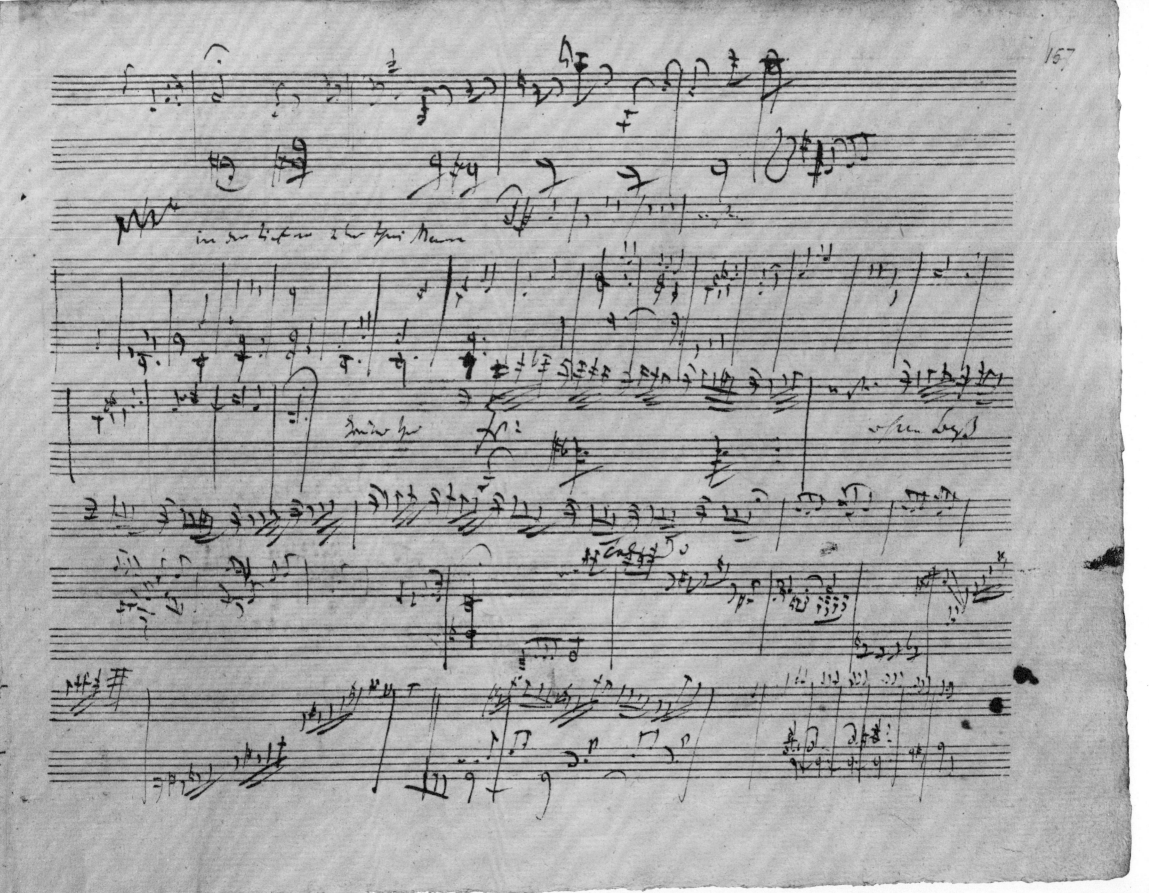

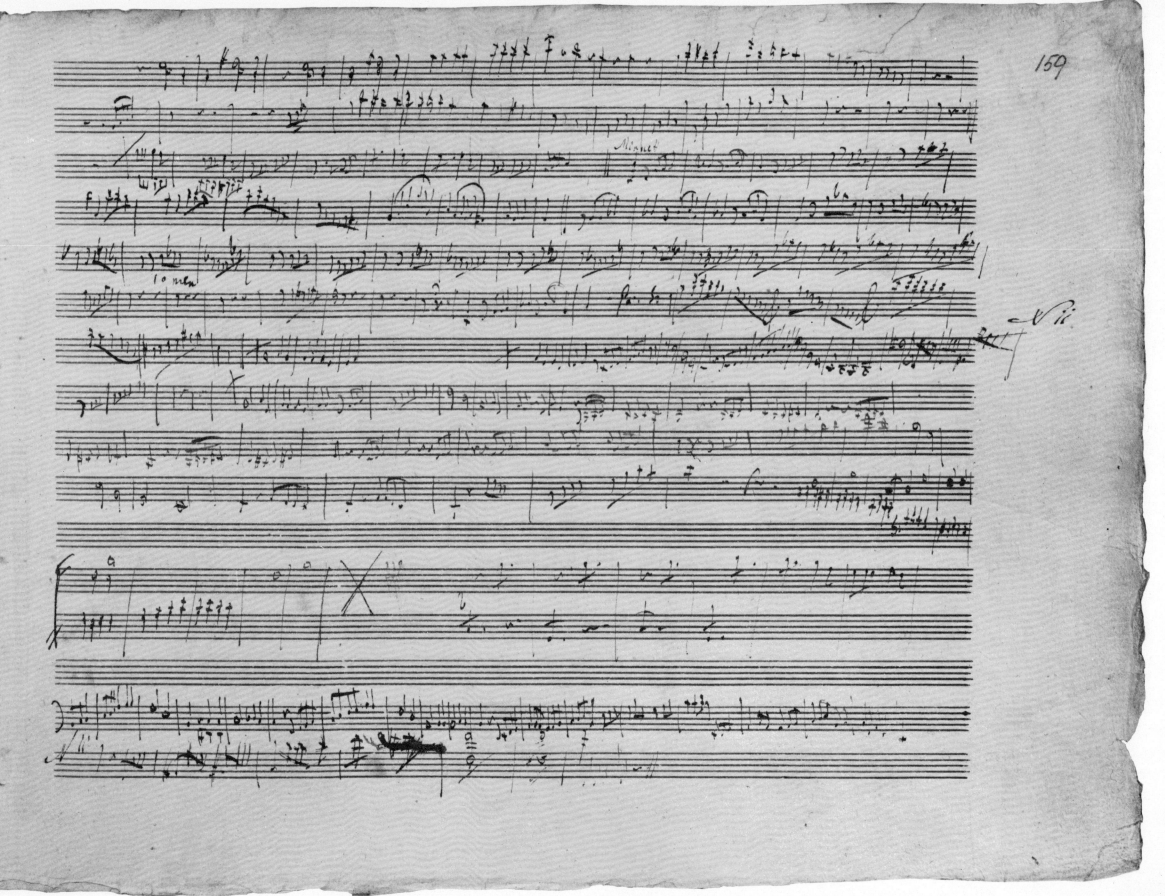

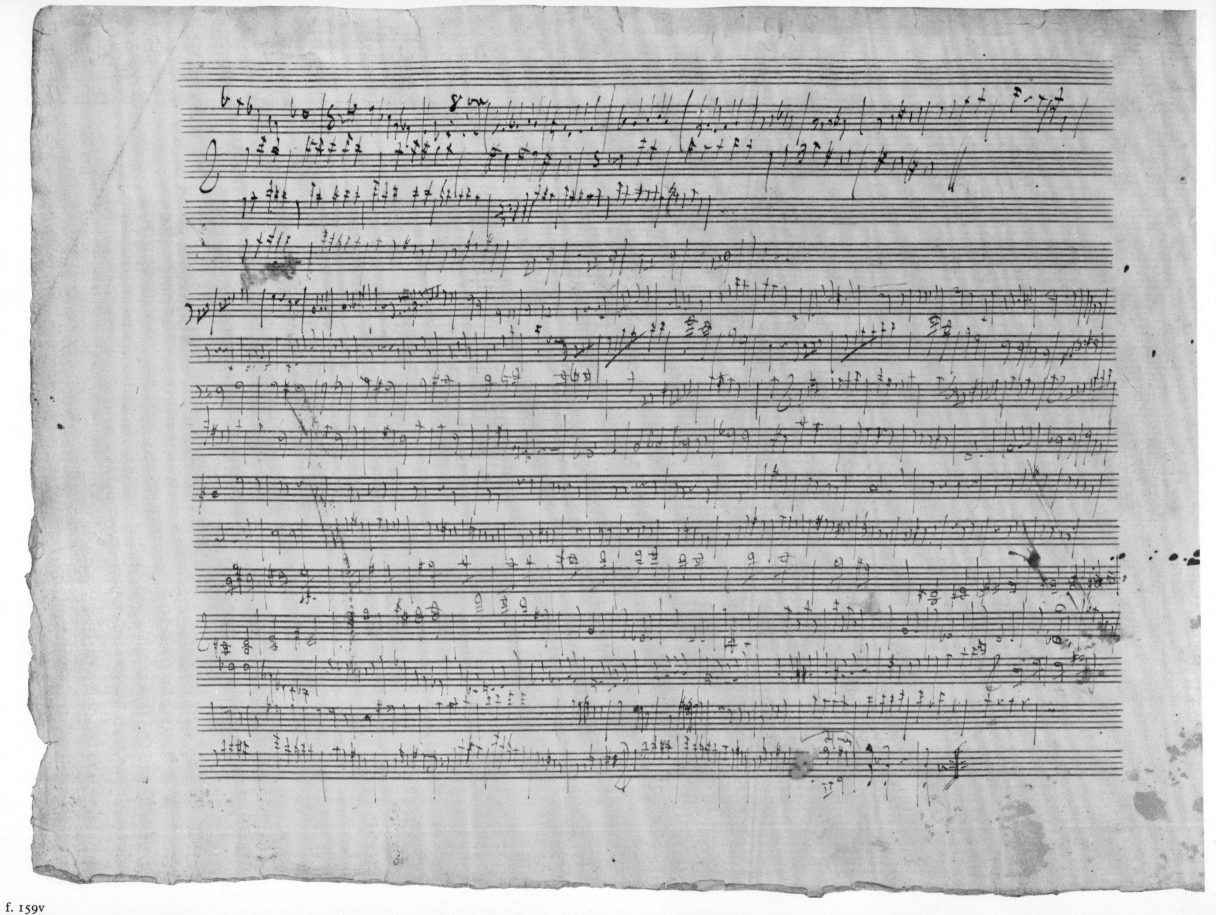

f. 161v

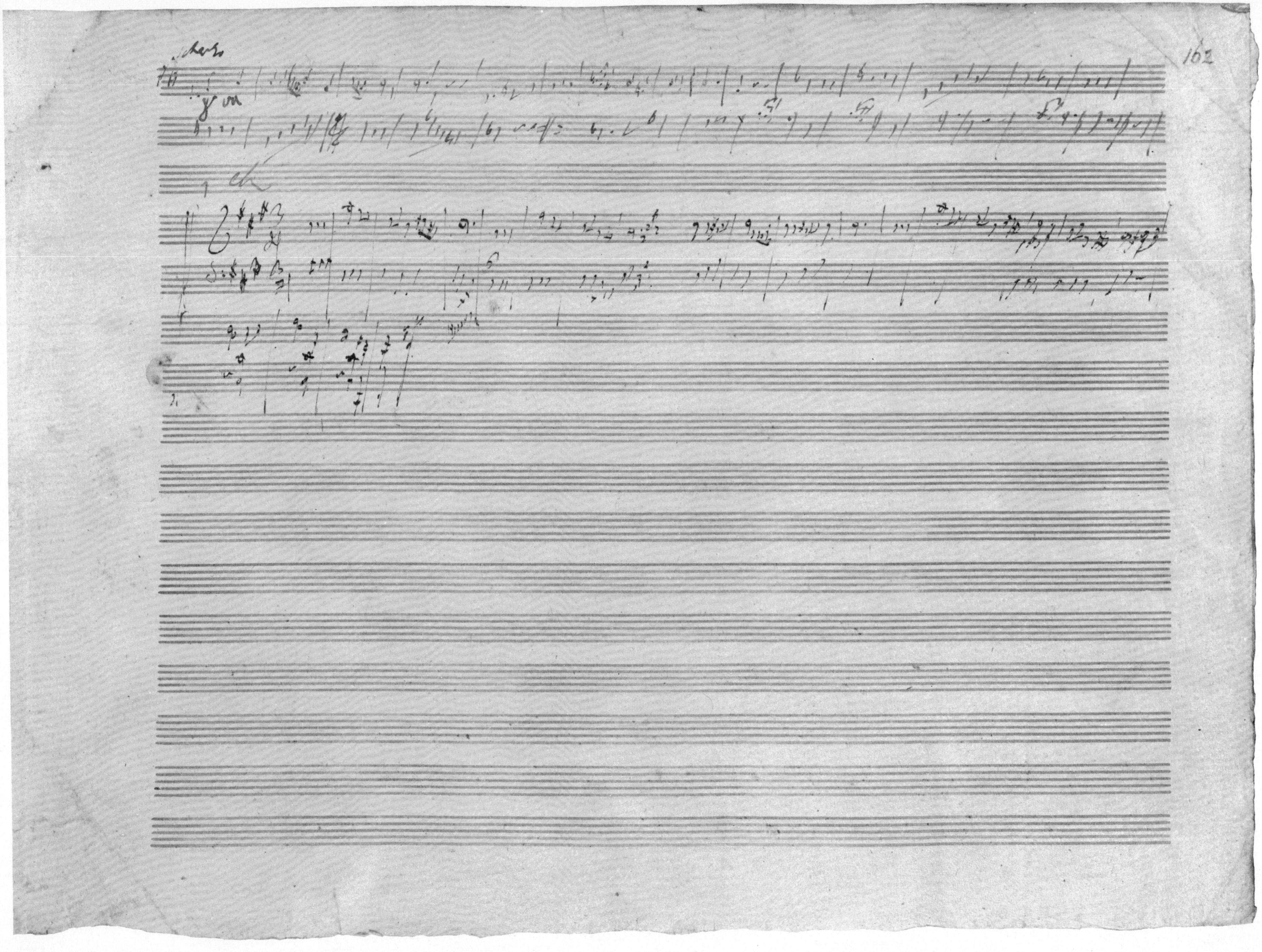

f. 162r